RAMON GUTHRIE'S
MAXIMUM SECURITY WARD

SALLY M. GALL

RAMON GUTHRIE'S
MAXIMUM SECURITY WARD

AN AMERICAN CLASSIC

A LITERARY FRONTIERS EDITION

UNIVERSITY OF MISSOURI PRESS

COLUMBIA, 1984

Library of Congress Cataloging in Publication Data

Gall, Sally M.
  Ramon Guthrie's Maximum security ward.

  (A Literary frontiers edition)
  Bibliography: p.
  1. Guthrie, Ramon, 1896–1973. Maximum security
ward. I. Title. II. Series.
PS3513.U875M334 1984   811'.52   83–16836
ISBN 0–8262–0430–9

  Selections from Ramon Guthrie's poetry copyright © 1968, 1969, 1970
by Ramon Guthrie and reprinted by permission of Persea Books, Inc.
from *Maximum Security Ward and Other Poems* copyright © 1984 by Sally
M. Gall.

  I owe a lasting debt of gratitude to M. L. Rosenthal, my friend and
collaborator, who introduced me to Ramon Guthrie's poetry and has
remained my most cherished consultant.

  What the dedication to my parents fails to record is the extraordinarily
open and inquisitive atmosphere they allowed me to breathe as a child:
a reflex in part of their roles as scientists, but even more of their
quintessential humanity.

  As always, I am deeply grateful to my husband for his enduring and
endearing interest in matters poetical.

S. M. G.
Suffern, N.Y.
September 1983

FOR MY PARENTS

BETTY C. AND JOHN A. MOORE

CONTENTS

Introduction

Late in 1970, precisely in the middle of two decades of self-indulgent American poetry, Ramon Guthrie's *Maximum Security Ward: 1964–1970*[1] was published. The finest achievement of a poet whose first books appeared in the 1920s but who found his most powerful voice in the 1960s, *Maximum Security Ward* took shape under intense psychological and physical pressure. Guthrie, in his seventies and struggling with cancer and a devastating sense of the betrayal by modern man of life's most generous possibilities, was able to transmute his disastrous condition into a beautifully articulated work of art.

A forty-nine-poem sequence, *Maximum Security Ward* was hailed at the time as "a seminal work of literature," a "deeply, heart-breakingly American book whose importance will become clearer and clearer as time passes," and "a fascinating work, and one of major character . . . like nothing else in contemporary poetry." Its immediate fate, however, was that of *Graffiti* and *Asbestos Phoenix*, Guthrie's two preceding volumes. It slipped quietly into obscurity. Still, in that radiant future when books written by twentieth-century poets will have sorted themselves out from books written by twentieth-century reputations, I firmly believe that *Maximum Security Ward* will be a star of honorable magnitude in a constellation glowing with such other classic sequences as *The Waste Land*, *Pisan Cantos*, and *Paterson*.

For *Maximum Security Ward* is not absolutely unlike anything else in contemporary poetry. It belongs to an increasingly formidable tradition, first treated in depth in *The Modern Poetic Sequence: The Genius of Modern Poetry*.[2] M. L. Rosenthal and I intended in that book to establish the pres-

1. New York: Farrar, Straus and Giroux, 1970; London: Sidgwick and Jackson, 1971; reprinted in *Maximum Security Ward and Other Poems*, edited by Sally M. Gall (New York: Persea Books, 1984).
2. By M. L. Rosenthal and Sally M. Gall (New York: Oxford University Press, 1983).

1

ence of this extraordinarily important genre and to trace its development from the mid-nineteenth century to the present. In a book treating sequences by some fifty poets—among them Whitman, Dickinson, Hardy, Yeats, Pound, Eliot, Williams, Crane, Olson, Stevens, Lowell, Berryman, Clarke, Plath, Hughes, Kinnell, and Rich as well as Guthrie—our discussion of *Maximum Security Ward* had, necessarily, to be curtailed.

This book, then, allows me to treat *Maximum Security Ward* in at least some of the depth it deserves, without believing for a moment that I have exhausted its multifariousness. Further, my book may serve to introduce to a wider audience a poet whose work as a whole is one of the joys of American literature. Born in 1896, Guthrie was in his sixties and had retired from the Dartmouth French department before he demonstrated how accomplished a poet he was. When he died on Thanksgiving Day 1973 at the age of seventy-seven, his poetry was still little known. Yet the poems of *Asbestos Phoenix* (Funk and Wagnalls, 1968), *Maximum Security Ward*, and to a lesser extent *Graffiti* (Macmillan, 1959), can serve as touchstones for the most important tendencies in postmodernist verse. Intensely personal and employing a fully contemporary idiom, they have the intellectual and emotional sweep, technical excellence, and truly organic structure we associate with the best writers in the British and American poetic traditions. That is, Guthrie was responsive to the whole range of psychological, physical, spiritual, social, and political pressures endemic to our war age; he had a superb ear; and he knew how to weld individual poems into a dynamic whole. Beyond all this, he was a uniquely humorous, lively, and engaging writer whose poetry is great fun to read.

With such a satisfyingly complex and developed artist, many essays from as many perspectives could be written on *Maximum Security Ward*. However, in a period when poetic criticism appears to be floundering in a morass of nonaesthetic concerns, it has seemed particularly important to emphasize the success of *Maximum Security Ward* as a unified work of art: to show how Guthrie used the freedoms and constraints of the sequence form to encompass and transcend the vast disarray of a lifetime's urgent experience.

In an opening note Guthrie himself stressed the interrelation of all the poems of *Maximum Security Ward*, perhaps rather pessimistic about whether it would be readily understood: "*Maximum Security Ward* is a single poem composed of a number of movements which, as often as not, are fully comprehensible only by their relation to the other movements and to the poem as a whole." Without a developed theory of the modern poetic sequence, "single poem" was one of the few terms available to him; however, the cumulative effect of the forty-nine poems of *Maximum Security Ward* demonstrates that Guthrie understood very well indeed the art of constructing a modern poetic sequence—and had the power, despite age and illness, to shape a brilliant one.

One reason for this high degree of achievement, and probably to some extent for the lack of sufficient critical attention during Guthrie's lifetime, has to do with his relatively late flourishing. Of the generation of MacLeish and MacDiarmid, Cummings and Graves, Crane, Tate, and Bunting, Guthrie had a respectable literary career as an expatriate poet and novelist based in France before he joined the Dartmouth French department in 1930. However, because he reached his full powers as a poet only in the 1960s, there has been no opportunity for the kind of sustained critical and scholarly attention that other poets of his generation have commanded.

Guthrie did have moments of recognition over the years, although not as many as his admirers would wish: fine reviews, a festschrift, and several poetry awards—including the 1970 Marjorie Peabody Waite Award of the National Institute of Arts and Letters. This $1,500 prize, "for continuing achievement and integrity in his art," was awarded in May, six months before the publication of what was to prove his most important book, *Maximum Security Ward*.

His long apprenticeship to his craft and his openness to the discoveries not only of his contemporaries and elders, especially Pound, but also of younger poets such as Auden and Lowell are matched by the extraordinary scope and maturity of his interests. *Maximum Security Ward* shows that he was at least as much at home on French as on American soil (he married a Frenchwoman, Marguerite Maurey, soon after the war); that his love of art embraced everything from cave paintings to Romanesque architecture to Beethoven to Proust to Robert Desnos; and that he took an innocent delight in esoterica of all sorts and in the play of mind and language.

In addition, an important quality of mature sensibility—rarer than one would wish—belongs to Guthrie's poetry. It is wisely, sympathetically, abundantly human and political in the best senses of the words. Guthrie searched deeply into the sources of suffering and into the wellsprings of human creativity, and his work is both artistically alive and comprehensive in its insight into the myriad facets of our human condition. Guthrie's art, like that of Rimbaud and his other christoi, "brings back secrets for changing life," and it does so nowhere more superbly than in *Maximum Security Ward*.

I. The Art of Sequence Making

One of the outstanding characteristics of *Maximum Security Ward* and of more ambitious sequences generally—*The Waste Land*, *Pisan Cantos*, *Paterson*, *The Maximus Poems*, *The Anathémata*—is the great variety they offer. We are likely to find many kinds and levels of language, sometimes conjuring up specific characters but often simply contributing to the shifting tonalities of the sequence. Rapid changes of scene and subject are routine, and allusions to other literary works abound. A sequence may attempt, more or less successfully, to ingest lyrics, jokes, brief narratives, meditative essays, dramatic scenes, sermons, curses, letters, prayers, diatribes, newspaper articles, reports—positively glorying in its mimicry of all the ways language has been used. The result may be a mélange of poetic and prose forms, confusing on the surface but beautifully comprehensible (if successful) once the essential structural principles of the genre are grasped. At that stage we can begin to compare the overall success of one sequence with another's, deciding, say, that *Maximum Security Ward* ranks with *The Waste Land*, the *Pisan Cantos*, and *Paterson* in its quality as a poetic sequence—and above Charles Olson's *The Maximus Poems* or David Jones's *The Anathémata*, impressive as the latter two works are.

There are many sequences in which the range of materials or variety of forms is not as strikingly wide as in the ones I have just mentioned but whose structural principles are essentially the same: for instance, Whitman's *Song of Myself*; Dickinson's fascicles; Hardy's *Poems of 1912–13*; Yeats's "Meditations in Time of Civil War," "Nineteen Hundred and Nineteen," *Words for Music Perhaps*, and his numerous other sequences; Eliot's *Four Quartets*; Stevens's "The Auroras of Autumn"; Auden's "Sonnets from China"; Crane's *The Bridge*; and Lowell's *Life Studies*. Since sequences have been with us so long and in many cases represent high points of modern poetry in English—and therefore have

5

been intensively studied—it would be very pleasant indeed to assume a general knowledge of their principles and move right on to a discussion of *Maximum Security Ward* as one specific instance of the genus *sequence*. However, since these works have seldom been studied for the way they work poetically, it may be useful to note the main structuring principles of the genre.

By and large, modern sequences are set off from conventional long poems in that their impulse is essentially lyric rather than logical, narrative, or dramatic—that is, they are not primarily concerned with argument or philosophical rumination, or with the tensions and expectations set up by the development of a plot, or with the dramatic immediacy of characters soliloquizing or interacting with each other. Rather, all these elements are subordinated to the creation of a lyrical dynamics: to the projection through language "wrought to its uttermost" of what Ezra Pound called "tones of mind" and what Rosenthal and I call "tonal centers" or "affects,"[1] involving everything we are capable of experiencing imaginatively, sensuously, emotionally, and intellectually. It is the lyric poet's business not only to create such moments in language but to shape them into a coherent whole as well, whether the work is a short lyric or a *lyric sequence*—a term we use interchangeably with *poetic sequence*. Thus, we find that despite all kinds of radical shifts of preoccupation, language, and style, despite the eschewal of most of the techniques of ordinary rational communication and of narrative and dramatic development (including especially the consistent characterization of a speaker or speakers), and despite the almost bewildering formal variety displayed in the typical modern sequence—despite all these, the best sequences *do* cohere.

Not all sequences, of course, are equally successful in presenting a satisfying curve of movement from beginning to end. But we are likely to find that the more inevitable a certain progression of the poems and passages within it feels, the more likely it is that they can be seen in relation

1. See in particular pages 6–11 of *The Modern Poetic Sequence*.

to some highly charged psychological state—a state of passionate awareness—that is complex enough to provide the motive force for all the strands of feeling running through the sequence. The sequence unfolds all the nuances of this state, sometimes rapidly, sometimes at a more leisurely pace, and as it does so we feel that there has been a psychologically valid development. The sequence starts *here* and ends *there* (achieving a kind of psychological balance rather than any firm intellectual resolution), and nothing in its course suggests that such an evolution would be impossible. More positively, it may even seem for the moment to have been inevitable.

*   *   *

Any sequence of real achievement contains individual poems so completely and superbly powerful by themselves that they irradiate all the others. In *Maximum Security Ward* such a key element is "Arnaut Daniel (circa 1190)," the thirty-ninth poem, which brilliantly incorporates a number of the strands of feeling animating the sequence. Its structure is worth examining closely; besides serving as a magnetic center for other passages in *Maximum Security Ward*, it epitomizes, on a small scale, the dynamics of the sequence as a whole. That is, it shifts from one tonal center to another, just as the sequence shifts from one kind of poem to another, in the familiar high modernist style we find in a typical canto by Pound, or in the first section of *The Waste Land*, or in a section of *Paterson*.

By the time we reach "Arnaut Daniel" in a continuous reading of the book, we have become familiar enough with Guthrie's lavish use of figures from myth and history that it seems quite natural for a twelfth-century troubadour to share a poem with Marsyas, with a Browning enthusiast who has some of Guthrie's own acid qualities, and with the chowderheaded Mr. Bodington, "President of the British Chamber of Commerce of Paris." In fact, one of the reasons for the accessibility of Guthrie's sequence—contrasted, say, to the *Pisan Cantos*—is this unusual proliferation of speaking characters. Although they are not developed in a dramatist's or novelist's sense, they provide easily comprehensible clues to the changing emotions and preoccupations of the sequence.

Shifts in language serve much the same purpose, and the Arnaut poem uses a Provençal epigraph:

> *Ieu sui Arnautz qu'amas l'aura*
> *E chatz la lebre ab lo bou*
> *E nadi contra suberna.*

Guthrie translates Arnaut's words as his second stanza ("Arnautz am I . . ."), linking the troubadour with Marsyas and thus suggesting two mutually exclusive versions of Arnaut's life as well:

> My name is Marsyas. Everyone has heard
> of how I challenged Apollo, my flute
> against his harp. Midas, whom we had agreed on
> as judge, gave *me* the prize. The Romans
> put my statue in their forum, symbolizing
> Liberty. My name is Marsyas. I bore away the prize
> over Apollo, god of music.
>
>   Arnautz am I.
> I reap the wind, ride an ox
> to course the hare and swim against the torrent.
>
> I am Marsyas. There is another version.
> This time the Muses—his stable—were the judges.
> When they gave *him* the prize,
> he trussed me to a tree, flayed me alive.
> Choose your own version. I am a crude,
> goat-footed, flute-playing, wineskin-sucking
> lout that would as soon
> screw a Muse as look at her. Sooner maybe.
> Depending how she looked.

These opening stanzas are more than a prelude to the body of the poem, which is a slangily tough, humorous, lyrical, and finally touching portrait of the aging troubadour. The first stanza has a brisk, colloquial boastfulness to it, a tone suitable for a successful artist who can whip his weight in gods and, immortalized, serves future generations as a model of the free human spirit. Then, as if we had stumbled into yet another contest for artistic honors, Arnaut offers in response *his* credentials. For the moment these appear to be somewhat dubious; his efforts as an artist have obviously not, in his opinion, been crowned by success. But in counterpoint to Arnaut's wryly pessimistic summation of his career is the simple fact that the lines themselves have endured, after all, for eight hundred years. The underside to creativity—the artist's sense of personal failure—is embodied at the beginning of the third stanza in the more common version of the Marsyas myth. Now, the contest has been rigged from the start by a powerful and vengeful god, who punishes human aspirations with a complete lack of justice or compassion. The flippant "Choose your own version" applies not just to this particular myth but to the innumerable choices postulated throughout *Maximum Security Ward*: questions of what to believe about one's own life, and human nature, and the course of human history.

In the last lines of the stanza, Guthrie suddenly reminds us that Marsyas was not man but satyr, and the rambunctiously raunchy language recaptures something of the tone of the boastful opening stanza and allows the poem to modulate adroitly to the first of five stanzas devoted to Arnaut:

> I, Arnaut Daniel, was born at Ribérac.
> I am one honest-to-God *good* poet.
> Parchment is dear. Most monks are lunks.
> Nobody else can read. What is there to do about it?
> *Niente*. Absolutely *nada*. A couple of years from now
> it will be spring again
> and I shan't be around to see it.
> Willows budding in the meadow, gentians,
> jonquils in the woods, girls twittering
> in patches of sunlight by the river,
> giggling and squealing and hiking up their petticoats
> thigh-high to wade ankle-deep trickles in the field,
> and I not be there. I've had this cough since Sicily,
> gone to make songs for Richard Lion-Heart.
> Ten years from now nobody will have heard of me.
>   Not only as a poet. *Shove poetry!*

One way or another, it has kept me eating
most of my life. But shove it all the same.
What I'll miss is girls stooping by the brook,
picking cowslips, raising their arms
to put them in their hair and show the sweet
profiles shaping out with spring.

We have moved out of the literary and mythical realm
and into daily life. As in *Maximum Security Ward* as a whole,
this poem is informed by the artist's urgent need, with
death approaching, to take stock of his life and work. (Note
how the image of violent death in the preceding stanza
prepares us for the references in this one—although they
are considerably less dramatic.) The opening tone is close
to that of the two Marsyas stanzas: the troubadour, too, is
perfectly confident of the worth of his achievement. But he
has a very human concern for the ultimate fate of his art,
conveyed by a splendid exasperation with his cultural mi-
lieu. In this world before the printing press, his reputation
is as chancy as Marsyas's. With the thought of the inevi-
table year that will arrive without him, however, Arnaut's
soliloquy changes character. Mixed in with his grumbling
is a bittersweet celebration of the joys of spring, including
his delight in the half-innocent seasonal wantonness of the
"twittering girls." And by the end of the stanza, the tone is
one of bemused rapture at the sexual promise in all those
"sweet profiles shaping out with spring" and of poignant
realization that it is this aspect of life that enthralls him
even more than the practice of poetry.

Arnaut, then, agrees with Marsyas—but in a much more
artistically refined way—that a poet should "as soon screw
a Muse as look at her." The energetically lyrical language
together with the spicy Marsyan vulgarity of the phrase
"Shove poetry!" connects this fourth stanza with the well-
springs of the most vital art. Such art depends—as Guthrie
and other magnificent old poets, Yeats and Williams for
example, knew so well—on both artistic craftsmanship and
a passionately sensuous and sensual alertness to whatever
the world has to offer.

The humorous veins of this poem, whether wry, bawdy,

or sardonic, coalesce in the sixth stanza as a sort of medieval traveling-salesman joke:

> Aï! given a few springs more and even the spawn
> of my own loins won't ever have heard my name.
> Their mammies will have told them,
> "Your pappy was a travelin' man," or
> "You are the offspring of a foreign dignitary
> who, hearing of my beauty, sent his emissaries . . . "

Still, the outcry is heartfelt and makes way for the most poignant stanza in the poem:

> Ieu sui Arnautz qu'amas l'aura.
> Today a brown dog lay sleeping in the sun
> outside the tavern. I said, "Hello, dog."
> Without bothering to open his eyes,
> he beat the warm dust with his tail.
> I am Arnaut. I shall be planted in the ground before
> that chestnut sapling first bears fruit.

So far have we come from "I am one honest-to-God *good* poet," and yet the undercurrent of desperation has been stressed throughout in the image of reaping the wind. When it appears here for the third time, it bears with it, as so many of Yeats's refrains do, the burden of all that has gone before. "Ieu sui Arnautz qu'amas l'aura" has shaped the poem, but Guthrie has not allowed his language to plunge into pathos. Even here, the dog's matter-of-fact response to Arnaut's greeting wards off sentimentality. The image itself is enough; there is an implied contrast, however, with the behavior of faithful Argos at the reappearance of his master, Odysseus, after twenty years: in the legendary case, expiration in a kind of ecstasy; here, friendly acknowledgment. The difference, of course, is similar to the one between Arnaut and Marsyas. At the end of his soliloquy, Arnaut opts for the mundane, for very human but nonetheless extraordinary achievements:

> If you want to see
> something of what my eyes have seen,
> go down to Moissac's abbey—the twenty-four
> Elders with their white robes and golden crowns

and burnished lutes and rebecs, the Christ in majesty,
the cloister. Moissac or Dalon or Cadouin
if they are still standing. Conques, Montsalvy.
Go down to Beaulieu in Dordogne;
the tympanum there shows the Last Judgment
with Jews lifting up their robes
to show the sign of their covenant with Jehovah.
I am Arnaut Daniel. I lived
in a not too unlovely world.

Here, in the poem's penultimate stanza, Arnaut draws
attention to the achievements of artists working in a differ-
ent medium and ostensibly in a different spirit: the makers
of the great Romanesque cathedrals, churches, and ab-
beys. Along with the flowers and girls of spring, these
religious monuments, in their beauty and robustly matter-
of-fact treatment of sexual matters—the "Jews lifting up
their robes / to show the sign of their covenant with Jeho-
vah"—make for a "not too unlovely world." The poem
suggests that the impulses of secular and religious art are
very close indeed—a point that *Maximum Security Ward* as
a whole demonstrates fully.

Arnaut's last words also raise the possibility of the de-
struction even of such substantial edifices, thus reminding
us of his anxiety about the fate of his own work. That such
places are also the haunts of those lunkish monks, who
exercised him so much several stanzas back, certainly sug-
gests a rigorous honesty in his aesthetic responses. He
understands and delights in artistic integrity in whatever
form it takes, unlike the priggish Mr. Bodington of the final
stanza. At the end of his soliloquy Arnaut addresses future
generations who may be lucky enough to see what his eyes
have seen, and a lesser poem might well have ended here.
Guthrie, though, brings us explicitly into the present (as
the language he has provided for Marsyas and Arnaut has
done implicitly) with a final sardonic stanza that skewers
narrowly moralistic and therefore completely misguided
perceptions of the nature of art:

Mr. Bodington, President of the
British Chamber of Commerce of Paris and

authority on Romanesque architecture of
central, south and western France, said,
"Browning was not a gentleman. I am surprised
you should have read him."
Questioned, he explained, "Why, the fellow was—
uh, no need to cite specific
instances—uh, vulgar, so to speak."
   (Something I must have missed.)

Mr. Bodington makes himself ridiculous on three counts. First, there is the complete irrelevance of either vulgarity or refinement, in themselves, to artistic achievement or as a criterion for choosing which poets to read; second, the questionable accuracy of describing Browning or his poetry as vulgar; and third, giving a special twist to Mr. Bodington's morally motivated opinions, his obvious blindness to the sensual content of the style of architecture on which he is supposedly an authority.

Aesthetically, what is one to make of a poem in which there are ostensibly four different speakers: a satyr from a mythical age; a troubadour from the 1100s; Mr. Bodington, the twentieth-century Victorian who specializes in the architecture Arnaut knew and loved; and the Guthrian speaker of the last line? The poem certainly owes something to Browning's dramatic monologues, but if we insist on consistent characterization it must be deemed both confusing and a failure. Since it is both clear and successful, however, we must obviously bring other criteria to bear. In fact, the principle of lyrical structure applies to individual poems as well as to whole sequences. There is a perfectly clear progression of feeling in "Arnaut Daniel (circa 1190)," and its variety of speakers is best viewed as a poetic technique for delineating varied states of feeling. Each speaker embodies a way of perceiving the world—quite complex and developed in the case of Arnaut, less so for the others. Since we are dealing with lyric poetry, not drama, speakers and characters do not have to interact directly—although the last stanza of this poem veers slightly toward the dramatic through the presence of Mr. Bodington and his questioner. In a lyric poem, the structure arises not from the interaction among identifiable characters but from the interaction of states of feeling as projected in language.

While a lyric poem or sequence does not need characters, speakers, or dramatic situations to justify its tonal shifts, they are potent resources and can help the reader to understand a poem more quickly. As we shall see, Guthrie draws on such devices from the very start of *Maximum Security Ward*.

II. IN THE KEY OF IMMEDIACY

Frequently the first poem of a sequence telegraphs the course of the whole work, although it rarely does so in the sense of giving an outline of what is to come. It may in fact provide a welter of images—hints and suggestions of intense feeling and of a life gone out of control. This creatively suggestive chaos contains possible starting points for a number of strands on which the rest of the poems in the sequence might hang, without projecting, at such an early stage, any final, unalterable design. This is certainly true, for example, of the opening passages of Pound's *Pisan Cantos*, not to mention the extremely long opening poem, Canto 74, itself. It is true of the first poem of Emily Dickinson's superb fascicle 15, "The first Day's Night had come";[1] of the first of the Crazy Jane poems, "Crazy Jane and the Bishop," in Yeats's *Words for Music Perhaps*; and of "The Going" at the start of Hardy's *Poems of 1912–13*. "Elegy for Mélusine from the Intensive Care Ward," which opens *Maximum Security Ward*, also provides very strong indications of the major preoccupations and tensions informing the sequence as a whole.

The first poem or section of a genuine sequence is usually marked by two special characteristics. First, it suggests feeling intense enough to generate successive poems; and second, it somehow prepares the way for the whole range of materials the poet will subsequently introduce into the sequence. The poem need not be the best or clearest in the sequence, nor does it need to be so complete in itself that it would be an anthologist's delight. Its business is to start things off, and it is frequently by hindsight only, after the sequence has been read through in its entirety and properly absorbed, that the first poem—or even poems—can be treated with sufficient accuracy.

1. See *The Manuscript Books of Emily Dickinson*, ed. R. W. Franklin (Cambridge, Mass.: The Belknap Press of Harvard University Press, 1981).

What strikes us at once about "Elegy for Mélusine from the Intensive Care Ward" is its sheer verve and directly personal tone:

> So name her Vivian. I, scarecrow Merlin—
> our Broceliande this frantic bramble of
> glass and plastic tubes and stainless steel—
> could count off such illusions as I have
> on a quarter of my thumbs.
>
> > (. . . *even a postcard of Viollet-le-Duc's*
> > *pensive chimera signed with her initial . . .*)
>
> I penciled out a cable: FCHRISAKE COMMA
> WRITE TO ME STOP YOURE LIVING AND IM DYING.
> Gray lady challenged the expletive and my assurance
> that it was an Ainu epithet of endearment.

By the end of the first two and one-half stanzas, then, the poem's wonderfully idiosyncratic language has conjured up a specific voice. We have, in fact, been introduced with commendable promptness to the presiding sensibility of the sequence: a thoroughly beleaguered old man whose mental state at the start matches his physical entrapment by all the paraphernalia of a modern intensive care unit.

Guthrie's choice of locale for his sequence was brilliantly apt, and he exploited its dramatic possibilities superbly—just as Pound twenty years earlier had drawn upon an actual maximum security encampment for some of the best effects in his *Pisan Cantos*. Guthrie's intensive care ward is not after all a ward in a prison or an insane asylum but one in an ordinary hospital. It does share enough characteristics with the other kinds of ward, however, that in subsequent poems—for example, the fourth, "Via Crucis"—he can call up the most drastic associations, using asylum and prison imagery to convey his disastrous psychological and physical condition with noteworthy poetic economy. Like *Pisan Cantos*, *Maximum Security Ward* has a biographical base: Guthrie's surgery for cancer of the bladder in 1966. Although he was in the intensive care ward for only a few hours of his hospital stay, it was long enough for a splendid poetic idea to take shape. He started on the book almost immediately, and a substantial first draft, dated July 1966 to November 1967, exists in the Dartmouth Archives.

The biographical data, however, have undergone a total aesthetic conversion. Thus, while the hospital experience remains absolutely believable at a personal level, Guthrie's selection and transmutation of the details give this particular intensive care ward powerful symbolic and universal significance. The conversion process is very similar to what Pound did with the Disciplinary Training Center near Pisa in his eleven-canto sequence; indeed, the two works illuminate each other effectively, with Guthrie's sequence making the sense of crisis and the associative process in Pound's much more immediately apprehensible.

But let us return to the "Elegy" and note how quickly Guthrie has translated a literal hospital scene into a mythical forest. In fact, the opening lines suggest a surprising number of the preoccupations and techniques of his sequence: the fluid boundary between the mythical and the human; age, loneliness, disillusionment, betrayal by a loved woman; the mingling of the simplest concerns (the longing for a letter) and reasonably erudite knowledge (the existence of the Ainu; the proper designation of the Notre Dame figure as a chimera, not a gargoyle); and the mixture of almost hysterical pleading and feisty humor. For the moment, questions of Mélusine-Vivian's reprehensible actions rather than of his own health are uppermost. The poem develops as a *cri de coeur* to this lady, who represents such a nadir in correspondents that even with her lover on the brink of death she would probably not be bothered to write.

Although no doubt based on a real woman, her names—Vivian, Mélusine—place her in an archetypal realm of French romance. Vivian, of course, was the young sorceress who "laid a spell on her elderly lover Merlin that was to keep him forever captive and visible only to herself," as Guthrie explains in his note on that "vast forest of Brittany," Broceliande. Other poems written during the prolific *Maximum Security Ward* period feature Merlin and Vivian. One imagines that, whatever the literal biographical facts, their legend corresponds rather closely to the way he perceived a personally devastating relationship. Mélusine, too, ranks as a bit of a sorceress, a shape-changing *fée* who on Saturday nights tended to turn into a snake from the waist down. (She was forced to desert her husband, Count Raymond— I doubt that the similarity between *Ramon* and *Raymond* is coincidental—when he violated her orders and discovered this interesting physiological quirk.) Her modern namesake appears first in *Asbestos Phoenix*, in a slightly different draft of the "Elegy" (*Asbestos Phoenix* contains four *Maximum Security Ward* poems) and in the superb "Alba for Mélusine." Far more than a simple celebration of Mélusine's charms after a night of love, the alba—the Provençal equivalent of the aubade—is as desolate in its way as the complementary "Elegy":

> Waking beside you I watch this night
> dissolve inexorable into dawn.
> I put words from me. No need of second sight
> to scotch the lie that seas are narrow,
> years short and bring no change.

The point is that when Mélusine, Vivian, a scarecrow Merlin, Broceliande, Viollet-le-Duc's pensive chimera, and a northern Japanese aboriginal tribe crop up within the space of one title and eleven lines, we should not assume a display of scholarly knowledge for its own sake. Each reference reverberates in a number of emotionally relevant ways. Even the Ainu, after all, are introduced with a practical purpose: to disarm a nurse (or perhaps a "gray lady" is a subdued version of a candy-striper?) enough to allow the missive to Mélusine to proceed with its desperation intact.

At the same time, such a welter of characters and realms and times and places has its own aesthetic impact. It is thoroughly witty and hilarious: any poet who can bolster his position with the alleged linguistic peculiarities of the Ainu deserves our expectant attention, even if the day goes to the "gray lady" ("I struck out everything but WRITE"). Actually, humor in a quieter form is present from the opening line. "So name her Vivian" is in part a variation on

Melville's famous "Call me Ishmael"; indeed, "Ishmael" turns out to be one of the names donned by the protagonist of *Maximum Security Ward*. (Ishmael and his mother were driven out by Abraham; at the age of three Ramon, his mother, and his sister were similarly deserted.) Even Merlin's wry self-designation as a "scarecrow" can be seen as a thoroughly apt allusion to Yeats's haunting image for an "aged man" in "Sailing to Byzantium," who is no more than "A tattered coat upon a stick, unless / Soul clap its hands and sing, and louder sing / For every tatter in its mortal dress." This might seem a slightly farfetched comparison, except that Guthrie, too—in "Arnaut Daniel (circa 1190)" and elsewhere—heartily applauds the study of what Yeats calls "monuments" of the soul's "own magnificence." Guthrie, however, can rarely stay as solemn as the Irish poet, so *his* monuments tend to have a quirky magnificence. Humor for our poet is obviously one of the soul's saving graces, and it is absolutely typical of him to take established forms such as alba and elegy and turn them on their heads.

After the altercation over "FCHRISAKE," the tone of this particular elegy takes on a more relaxed and introspective cast—with the exception of the fervent prayer to two ladies who might be presumed to have some influence over the activities of a Frenchwoman:

> I struck out everything but WRITE—cheaper
> and besides I wasn't really dying
> save that I couldn't breathe too well
> nor feed except on intravenous dextrose.
>
> Still stands that I am dying, Mélusine,
> and have been ever since my infancy,
> but the process is more measurable now.
> You can tick off the months on a calendar—
> eeny, meeny, miny . . . and when you get to the end . . .
>
> > (*Today again no word.*
> > *. . . Breton Saint Anne . . . Black Virgin*
> > *of Le Puy . . .*)

The first five stanzas focus on an actual dramatic situation: a patient hitched up to various kinds of lifesaving apparatus and yearning desperately for any communication from his absent mistress. Guthrie then takes a slight risk, devoting more than half the poem to the macabre fantasy of a funeral with a talkative and disillusioned corpse eager to shock his mourners with the news that he has always hated living. For all but the most unsympathetic reader this strategy works, because the language remains sufficiently lively: "when I am tucked and snug and smug"; "I'd like to give one last galvanic jerk / and flip up straight"; "from the moment when / my drunken Uncle Doc dangled me by the heels / and whacked my rump"; "Every tear would dry like sizzled spit / testing a hot flatiron"; "'Why, the old bastard! Who'da thunk it of him!' / (It would be no time for grammatical niceties)." The crisply alliterative style reaches a peak in the description of "high-stepping young / Drum Majorettes with the minniest of Miniskirts," who are twentieth-century equivalents of Arnaut Daniel's lasses "hiking up their petticoats / thigh-high," and in the opening line of the next-to-last stanza:

> Fell fable of the fox that did at last
>   leap high enough and the grapes
>   definitely *were* sour.
>
>   (. . . *or an empty envelope addressed in her concise*
>   *swift runic hand.*)

The poem ends with a phrase—"concise / swift runic hand"—lovely enough to suggest that *Maximum Security Ward* will offer passages of high lyricism in addition to all its other tonalities. This note is particularly welcome after the somewhat self-conscious, slangy swaggering of the immediately preceding stanzas. Guthrie thus performs a delicate balancing act in "Elegy for Mélusine from the Intensive Care Ward." It is a poem whose linguistic flexibility prepares us very well indeed for the sequence as a whole, unless, of course, we allow ourselves to be put off (as Mr. Bodington no doubt would be) by momentary vulgarities. Like everything else in the sequence, vulgarity has an aesthetic purpose, serving to keep us in touch with that healthily common and very human coarse reality that prevents art from becoming pedantically cerebral and attenuated. (Hence, Marsyas's dual attitude toward muses, springing from his dual nature as satyr and musician.) There is, however, a question of proportion, and Guthrie will purposely use a low style to suggest some radical disorientation of a speaker's psyche. The "Elegy," then, projects a need to regain psychological equilibrium—indeed, the entire sequence is in large part a search for such equilibrium.

However, we should not confuse Guthrie's projection of a limited, perhaps desperately confused psychological state with his poetic craftsmanship. That is, the vocabulary and general tone may suggest such a sensibility, but the language is crafted with careful attention to sound values. When we examine even the most colloquial of Guthrie's lines—say, "my drunken Uncle Doc dangled me by the heels"—we find that it is highly rhythmical and uses alliteration, assonance, and even irregular internal rhyme effectively. This line turns out, in fact, to be iambic hexameter with a central caesura followed by a logically appropriate foot reversal ("dangled"). Naturally, such rigorous attention to metrics adds to the humor of the image, as does the alliteration on *d*, the assonance of *me* and *heels*, and the rhymes *my/by* and *drunk/Unc-* (not to mention the subtle repetition of *l*, the chiming of the *nk*, *nc*, and *ng* sounds, and the shift from predominately back vowels in the first half of the line to front vowels in the second).

Another aspect of Guthrie's balancing act is very much worth noting. The effect of parody, burlesque, and allusion in the hands of a sophisticated poet is rarely simple. Such devices, to use an obvious metaphor, provide a highly suggestive contrapuntal line to the dominant melody. The image of the baby dangling by its heel—especially since the line is hexameter, even if the language is English—might possibly remind us of a certain tale of Achilles and his heroic enterprise. Again, the invocation of St. Anne and the Black Virgin of Le Puy cuts two ways, since they are being asked to intervene in what to the outside world is hardly a significant problem. In the one case, a possibly epic allusion suggests the exaltation of the mundane; in the other, calling in the Virgin and a saint in connection with a letter suggests a possible overstatement of the patient's degree of suffering. Or if the implied allusion to "Call me Ishmael" in "So name her Vivian" conjures up the archetypal outcast, the addition of the epithet "scarecrow" reduces Merlin to a lesser conjurer. From the start, then, the sequence projects the duality embodied in "Arnaut Daniel" by the two versions of the Marsyas legend: man as mortal and immortal, as absurd sufferer and magnificent creator.

*　　*　　*

After the opening "Elegy" there are a number of ways that the sequence might have developed. The next few poems might, for example, reasonably be expected to fill in all sorts of personal details about the protagonist's illness—a twentieth-century version of W. E. Henley's *In Hospital*, perhaps. Or, because much of the psychological distress seems attributable to Mélusine's behavior, we might be told considerably more about the ins and outs of their relationship. Or the sequence might start to clear up the question of just why life has remained one of those "acquired tastes you somehow can't acquire— / like some wines (Tokay, Monbazillac) / or foods (gazpacho, prune whip, lemon pie)." What actually happens is that Guthrie establishes in the next five poems an atmosphere of radical disorientation that accompanies acute psychological and physical pain. With the exception of the urgently direct "Today Is Friday," this atmosphere is accomplished primarily through Guthrie's flair for dark humor and through his powerful manipulation of the anchoring metaphor: the intensive care ward perceived as a maximum security ward.

"Red-Headed Intern, Taking Notes," is a brief and bizarre coda to "Elegy," its magnificently jumbled language ("Speakless, can you flex your omohyoid / and whinny ninety-nine?") complementing the opening poem's "frantic bramble of / glass and plastic tubes and stainless steel."

The intern's zany questions—which culminate in "No history of zombi-ism in the immediate family? / And tularemia? No recent intercourse / with a rabbit?"—provide an exquisite parody of the bemusingly irrelevant questions any patient is liable to be asked on admission to a hospital. There is a grimmer side to all this, however, expertly underlined by references to being "speakless," to the patient's "phobia of spiders," to "zombi-ism," and to cheerfully brutal medical procedures:

> (Nurse, clamp the necrometer when I say when.
> If he passes out, tickle his nose with a burning feather
> and tweak his ears counterclockwise.)
> . . . .
> (Lash him firmly to the stretcher
> and store him in the ghast house for the night.)

The suggestions, after all, are of torture, imprisonment, madness, and death, and the poem finely captures the bewildered panic of a human being in pain who, cut off from the familiar and loved, feels more victim than patient. We are thus somewhat prepared for the third poem, "Today Is Friday," which is one of the most effective poems in *Maximum Security Ward*. The 1966–1967 draft of the sequence, in fact, opened with this terrifying evocation of pain and fear:

> Always it was going on
> In the white hollow roar
> you could hear it at a hundred paces if you listened closely
> and a hemisphere away if you didn't listen at all
> if you were paying no attention to it
> fixing your mind hard on something else
> > I will not hear it
> > I will not hear it
> > I
>
> Screaming it inwardly so hard it seemed
> your seminal vesicles must rupture with the strain
> you could hear it close at hand
> feel it crimping your nerve ends
> your brain pan buckling in its grip

23

Part of what this poem accomplishes is the successful embodiment of a "measurable" process of dying. In "Elegy" the patient indulges in a relatively mild counting-out rhyme for choosing the month of death ("You can tick off the months on a calendar— / eeny, meeny, miny . . . "). "Red-Headed Intern," too, has its savagely humorous way of measuring the degree of deadness—at least one presumes that a "necrometer" is not an instrument for measuring life processes. "Today Is Friday," however, is concerned not with measurement but with immediate, horrified apprehension of an "it" that has totally overwhelmed the patient's mind and body. The last image of this inexorable process is a ruthlessly vivid correlative for the information in "Elegy" that the patient "couldn't breathe too well":

Tangible
It is a great protracted
totally transparent cube
with sides and angles
perceptibly contracting against
eyeballs and nose and mouth and skin

It is always happening
It is always going on
When it gets tired of going on
maybe it will stop

Guthrie's title for his next poem, "Via Crucis," like "Today Is Friday," reminds us of a day of agony two thousand years ago, although "Via Crucis" is hardly a re-creation of the crucifixion. Nor does it make any specific comparisons, except a rather humorous one, between that archetypal victim and this hospital patient. Instead of the road to Calvary, the scene is merely a bathroom with all the stalls occupied:

Out of this   coming sidewise   slinking and
        sidling two steps forward and nine or ten
backward for fear of getting a charge of rock-salt
for a Peeping Tom . . . Gangway, lady! Gangway!
I'm doing a via crucis.
And she says, "B'jazes, it's the first time I ever seen

anybody doing one
in a hospital johnny! What are you—
a furriner or something?"
        Thou sayest it, lady. All these years
I've been wondering what I am and now I know:
        a foreigner or something. No kith, belike,
or kin of anything—at least among the higher primates—
a, biologically speaking, sport!

Guthrie uses this hilarious encounter between patient and Irish Catholic "lady" to introduce explicitly one of the basic preoccupations of *Maximum Security Ward*: the absolutely devastating loneliness felt by someone who believes he is "no kith, belike, / or kin of anything." Indeed, the drive to overcome this sense of radical isolation and terrifying uniqueness appears so often and in so many different guises in the sequence that we should probably view it as central to the work's dynamics. For the moment, however, Guthrie is more concerned with setting the scene, both literally and symbolically. The intensive care ward swarms with the activities of interns, doctors, and especially nurses: the "swift square-bottomed" one who "flits sure / from bed to bed, takes blood pressures and pulses, / checks drains and bandages, switches on chest pumps"; the "small wren-faced" one, clipboard in hand, checking on religious affiliation ("'I have to ask you just in case.' None. / She marks the X at Protestant"); and especially the "staff nurse," Mr. Goldblatt, a petty torturer who is too free with rectal thermometers and too stingy with water:

Come on, ol' sport, roll over so I can insert . . .

        "Look here, ol' sport,
I give you ginger ale a while ago.
You'da been thirsty, you'da drunk it
instead of yammerin' for water now.
You don't like ginger ale, it ain't my fault.
I'm busy now, I got my records to keep up."

Mr. Goldblatt contributes notably to the "maximum security" aspect of the hospital ward, but the physical characteristics of the ward and, above all, the critically injured and ill who inhabit it trigger the comparison. In this poem Guthrie suddenly transports us to a realm of brutality reminiscent of the atmosphere conjured up by Hogarth and other artists who specialize in depicting the depths of human misery and degradation. At the very least this ward belongs in a war zone:

> MR. GOLDBLATT: STAFF NURSE (white letters on
> blue plastic badge) buzzing like an officious
> bottlefly doing an imitation of Schnozzle Durante,
> struts in by what, if they would give me back my watch,
> must now be morning. There are no windows though
> to judge that by, only these cones of light
> trained on our eyelids . . . high iron grills
> fencing in each of the nearly touching beds
> constantly being (one man dying or making guggling
> sounds of death, another in new-bloodied bandages
> arriving) trundled in or out.
> . . . .
> Maximum Security Ward. Sure, I know . . .
> Intensive Care Ward, but none the less,
> straight out of Jacques Callot by Hogarth.

This passage is the most drastic description of the ward until we come to "'Loin de Moi . . . ,'" which is the climactic poem of part 1 and turns the whole world—especially "these United States"—into a gigantic death house. Such brutal realism is only one of several notes struck in "Via Crucis," however, which ends with a mock-heroic vision of revenge:

> MR. GOLDBLATT, you cloacal breathed, glad-handing ghoul,
> if ever I get my white
> corpuscles out of hock
> and temperature down enough to take it orally,
> I'm going to vault that side rail and ram
> those outsized, clicking dentures down your throat,
> God be my witness. SELAH.

This whimsical moment of wish fulfillment is precipitated by our hero's complete inability to prevent any of the indignities to which he is being subjected. He is definitely up against a situation over which he has no physical control; nevertheless, he can still call into play his relatively dauntless spirit, his teeming imagination, and his ability to draw wild analogies with other underdogs. For example, in the next poem, "Cadenza," his consciousness is concocted of equal parts of Marsyas, the ram sacrificed in Isaac's stead, Ishmael, and an ordinary uncomfortable patient. Marsyas is mentioned here for the first time, in a dialogue somewhat reminiscent of "Red-Headed Intern, Taking Notes" both in its catechistic quality—"Come on, name of mother?"—and in its word play. For example, "Marsyas" is introduced as one-half of a palindrome:

> "My name is Marsyas,"
>   says ram
> says ram to Abraham
> caught in the thicket by the horns.

The "square-bottomed" nurse from "Via Crucis" reappears in this fifth poem. Compared with Mr. Goldblatt, she is a ministering angel, and all things, including her handling of the vernacular, can be forgiven her:

>   "You comf'table? You don't look it.
> You want I should see if I could do
> sumpen about those pillows before I go?"

She is, after all, the first human being who has shown any compassion toward the patients in the ward, and at the most mundane level she is the first in Guthrie's "gamut of goddesses." These appear in the pivotal sixth poem, "Scene: A Bedside in the Witches' Kitchen," which gathers together many of the major motifs of the first five poems and launches us toward a more orderly world of memory and meditation. Guthrie's earlier books and a number of his unpublished poems reveal his exuberant delight in manufacturing the kind of nonsensical jargon of "Red-Headed Intern, Taking Notes," and the first stanza of "Scene" continues in this mode. After the brief episode with the kindly nurse, the sequence also returns us to the realm of cheerful sadism of which Mr. Goldblatt is the tutelary deity:

DOCTOR *to his retinue of interns and residents*:
> Obvious ptoritus of the drabia.
> Although the prizzle presents no sign of rabies,
> note this pang in the upper diaphrosis.
> When kicked there hard enough, the patient utters,
> "Yoof!" and curls up like a cutworm.

There is of course a serious side to such wordplay—the suggestion of mutual incomprehension on the part of patient and caretakers—and the second stanza, "PATIENT *to Nurse*" builds on this motif. The "foreigner" of "Via Crucis" turns out to be very strange indeed:

> My name is Marsyas, a stranger here.
> > How to explain?
> Sprächen zoo something? anything? Aard-vark? Gnu?
> you look well-meaning. If I made noises in my phlarynx
> and shaped them with my phtongue, would they have
> snignifigance to you?

Having identified the patient with Marsyas, Guthrie no longer needs a specially coined language to emphasize the extreme disparity between the patient and other human beings. This, then, is the last such passage in the sequence; from here on, references to the musician-satyr and his fantastically alien world can serve as reminders of the patient's radical isolation.

Not only is Marsyas a mythical creature, but even his mythical realm is relatively unfamiliar. A performer on the flute, not the lyre, and with strongly orgiastic origins, he belongs to the matriarchal tradition that was to be superseded by Apollo and the other classical gods. His art was dedicated to the earth goddess Cybele, so the invocation of a "gamut of goddesses" is particularly apt—after a brief reminder of the Christian tradition that in its time superseded the classical tradition:

> Today is Friday.

> Gamut of goddesses, Gaia, Latona, Frigg whose day it is,
> cat-flanked Ishtar with the up-turned palms,
> Rosmertha of the Gauls, with grief-gouged eyes
> and rough-hewn cleft—

sister, mother, mistress of the dead,
mare-shaped Epona, you, Venus of Lespugue
in mammoth tusk, majestic at scarce a handsbreadth tall,
though not quite small enough to put into a matchbox
and walk the streets of Montparnasse with in your
    pocket . . .

Gamut of goddesses,
in your spare moments intercede for me . . .
    (Breath comes scant now,
      but by chance you may have heard,
        my name is Marsyas) . . .
intercede for me. Let me be never born.
Let my ghost wander in brambled upland meadows.
Drizzle in evening streets, may she at times recall
our walking there, arms pressed to ribs together.

Mélusine!

This passage is one of the more notable invocations of
female deities in modern poetry, at the same time that it
contributes splendidly to the forward momentum of the
sequence and keeps alive many of the tonalities presented
in the preceding poems. Besides the reminder of the kinds
of torture associated in *Maximum Security Ward* with Friday,
there is the rather salacious—but irreproachable, in a
scholarly sense—reference to the day's nominal divinity,
Frigg. The mention of "scant" breath carries us back to the
suffocating imagery of "Today Is Friday," as well as to the
opening "Elegy" ("save that I couldn't breathe too well").
And the desperate plea to Mélusine in that first poem is
made more immediately comprehensible by the quick evo-
cation of magic times with her in "brambled upland mead-
ows" and "evening streets." It is particularly notable that
the litany of goddesses is more than a list of names; it is an
eclectic catalog of sculptures that have endured through
the centuries, even since paleolithic times ("you, Venus of
Lespugue"). However, it is a modern artist, Giacometti,
who leads us into the main body of *Maximum Security Ward*.

III. The Mode of Memory

"Montparnasse . . . " and "'Side by Side,'" the seventh and eighth poems, are the first of a number scattered through the book that keep it firmly anchored in Guthrie's personal experience. Whatever identities this mercurial patient has been appropriating for himself—Merlin, galvanized corpse, "old bastard," ghast house denizen, foreigner, "ol' sport," Marsyas, sacrificial ram, Ishmael, worshipper, ghost—the presiding sensibility is that of the historical Ramon Guthrie. The numerous biographical details the sequence provides may not always be absolutely accurate (there is no reason why they should be), but they jibe closely enough with what we know of Guthrie's life from sources outside the poems that we feel he is giving us an authentic portrayal of how he has lived and thought and felt over the course of a great many years.[1]

Fortunately, he is eminently worth listening to in his role as reminiscer and sage; and, besides, his poems are always far more than a self-indulgent return to the days of yore. Thus Montparnasse not only is a place to which he can never return—either in time or in space—but in the person of the sculptor Giacometti it also represents a whole way of perceiving the world. Giacometti is the first of Guthrie's "christoi" (as he will name them in the twenty-fourth poem): human beings who have broken through in their own ways to fresh and enduring affirmations of the human spirit. Typically they are unaware of their achievements or even seem actively to embrace the death principle. Thus Giacometti feels his art has not grown in fifty years and consumes enough Gauloises to assure his eventual death by lung cancer. The vignette of Giacometti at work and holding forth on life as essentially a passive sui-

1. Used judiciously, *Ramon Guthrie Kaleidoscope*, ed. George E. Diller, is a good source of biographical material. See also Sally M. Gall, "The Poetry of Ramon Guthrie."

cide is framed by some utterly desolate, highly personal stanzas. At the opening, there is the terrible sense that one has outlived one's time:

> Montparnasse
> that I shall never see again, the Montparnasse
> of Joyce and Pound, Stein, Stella Bowen,
> little Zadkine, Giacometti . . . all gone in any case,
> and would I might have died, been buried there.

Other poems, memoirs, and a portrait of Guthrie by Stella Bowen witness to the accuracy of this stanza's air of intimacy with the expatriate Parisian world between the wars. The impetus of the poem, however, is not self-puffery (*I was there and knew so-and-so*) but the realization that one's life has failed to meet one's own expectations. The slightly cryptic closing stanza, with its allusion in French to sexy-eyed ladies who are both beckoning and indifferent, is a long echo across the years to the goddesses who visited Pound in his tent in the Disciplinary Training Center near Pisa:

> Venus of flesh . . .
>   (Landing at Naples:
>   Colonel Bill's curly-headed
>   unpanted daughter panting for the plane.)
> *Au fond* perhaps   of limited lascivity . . .
> *Les yeux cernés, tendres mais sans la moindre tendresse.*

The references to Naples and Colonel Bill ("Wild Bill" Donovan, Guthrie's boss in the Office of Strategic Services during World War II) resonate more fully after we have read the whole sequence and are able to link this passage with other memories of World War II; in fact, there is a brief allusion to the same period in the next poem, during a recital of close shaves with death ("Just seven as I make it"): "Once Naples to Algiers / flying the deck—that hungry waterspout." This method of quick "spotting" of motifs is typical of *Maximum Security Ward* and does serve to emphasize the poems' common contexts, no matter how different they are in specifics. Thus, the riddling allusion in the sixth poem to walking through the streets of Montparnasse with a matchbox containing a piece of sculpture is promptly clarified in the seventh poem as Giacometti's casual "carrying about / his work of four whole years in half-a-dozen / matchboxes scattered through his pockets." And the reference to the "hungry waterspout" in the eighth poem will be picked up in the twentieth (the last poem of part 1), "Boul' Miche, May 1968," and finally clarified in the thirty-seventh poem, "For Approximately the Same Reason." The gamut of goddesses, too, now that they have been introduced, will reappear throughout the sequence in their own persons or embodied in other female figures, each time providing richer and richer resonances.

Two slightly different techniques are at work here. In the first case, that of partial revelation, each preliminary reference tends to float free of the lines surrounding it, its mysteriousness investing it with special importance. We are made to feel that the reference must represent a memory or an area of concern so constant in the poet's psyche that he sees no need for a special introduction. If our curiosity is sufficiently piqued, we shall read on with an eye toward solving a little mystery; that is, our engagement with the work will become more active. A subtle pattern of expectation and fulfillment has been introduced. What is required for the technique to work is a Keatsian "negative capability": the reader must be content to remain in "Uncertainties, Mysteries, doubts, without any irritable reaching after fact & reasons."

Naturally, a reader's memory must be reasonably alert for partial revelation to have full effect; and such readiness is necessary as well for the second technique, repetition with variation. In this process, for each repetition to acquire increasing depth and complexity, one must of course remember where, and in what form, the motif has appeared previously. Again, there must be active engagement on the reader's part. (One wonders if much of the supposed difficulty of modern and contemporary poetry stems from these hardly onerous demands on patience and memory.) There is the further problem of private reference in much recent poetry, which also demands negative capability in that we must be aware that we probably don't need all the biographical facts to grasp a slightly obscure passage: the basic need is to be alive to the experiential complex projected by the language. Of course, if a passage yields nothing at all to a sympathetically alert reader, then the poet is at fault for not having successfully converted personal experience into art. The problem, incidentally—to continue with some of the difficulties of modern poetry—is essentially the same with any kind of special knowledge, in the sciences or the humanities or any realm of human experience. The poet must give his material enough of a spark so that it can stand to some extent alone; that is, it should make emotional and intellectual sense even if we do not recognize every single reference. Naturally, a particularly interesting poem may well impel us to track down the unfamiliar—to educate ourselves, in fact. Then we, the poem, and civilization will have been served so much the better.

Guthrie in this sense, like Pound, is one of the true teachers. His language is powerful enough to make us want to know more about the people and events and discoveries and artifacts and beliefs that *Maximum Security Ward* suggests are particularly significant for understanding who we are and where we are going. Since Montparnasse is the first historical locale introduced besides the intensive care ward, it is probable that communities of artists might well have a certain importance in defining what it means to be human. Then, reinforcing the war-zone imagery of "Via Crucis," comes "'Side by Side,'" in which we are transported back to World War I. (The juxtaposition of these two poems, incidentally—apart from their particulars—is a model of two poles of the sequence: humanity's creative and destructive sides, with the vulnerable sensibility balanced between them, passionately loving and admiring the one and hating and distressed by the other.)

"Little of fellowship here," Guthrie remarks ironically at the opening of "'Side by Side,'" and his memory throws up a time when there was a certain sturdy fellowship in facing death. In World War I Guthrie drove an ambulance in the Balkans with the Armée de l'Orient and then in France. When the United States entered the war, he joined the U.S. Army's aviation signal corps. He trained at Aulnat, an airfield near Clermont-Ferrand, as an observer. On his second flight, the plane—a Sopwith—had mechanical trouble at one thousand feet and crashed in a marsh. He and his pilot walked away, but afterward Guthrie was bothered with migraine, acusis—low tolerance for loud noise—and amnesia (see the forty-fifth poem, "'Visse, Scrisse, Amò'").

While serving in the Eleventh Bombing Squadron, Guthrie shot down four enemy planes in the three months before the armistice and earned a silver star—which he returned to President Johnson in protest against the Vietnam War. In *Kaleidoscope*, George Seldes graphically describes the primitive conditions under which U.S. airmen were sent aloft: with machine guns out of order, without parachutes, and in dangerous De Havilland Fours that were little more than flaming coffins. Seldes, who was with the press corps, explains that the rationale for the brutal callousness of the officers was that America was "lousy with aviators." The imagery of flaming planes in "Death with Pants On" (the thirty-sixth poem) comes from direct experience, but at the time Guthrie was curiously untouched by fear. Perhaps falling out of the sky but, unlike Icarus, surviving—see "Icarus to Eve," the twenty-second poem— made him feel immortal.

In "'Side by Side'" the illusion is a concomitant of youth:

> I do not count that afternoon nor would
> if the fuse itself had struck
> square on my cranial suture, death no more
> real for me than for the fool squirrel
> racing to throw a body block
> on an oncoming truck.
>> Too young to think that we could ever die.

Guthrie is recalling an incident one afternoon at Flirey when he and other ambulance drivers had their game of chess rudely interrupted by a shell and the death of a player who was a bit late into the dugout. That insouciantly fearless Guthrie, unable to imagine himself as a corpse although he so nearly was one, contrasts markedly with Marsyas-Guthrie some fifty years later, considering the disposition of his remains in humorously gruesome detail:

> Should I have willed my corneas?
> My old but still staunch heart?
> my cadaver *in toto*? Medical schools will pay
> good money in advance for a second-hand cadaver.
>
> No! not to have my brine-shriveled scrotum
> bandied about, my epididymis unraveled, measured by
> some embryo Bovary.

The uneasy sexual emphasis is reinforced by the line "I don' wan' me bollicks shot awy-y-y," from a popular World War I marching song, and by the anecdote of the Cockney soldier who has suffered precisely this wound and asks for a gun to finish himself off. Guthrie's own catalog of brushes with death, excluding the incident at Flirey when he was as unconscious of death as any nonhuman animal ("This Stealth" proposes an awareness of death as the distinguishing human characteristic) is offered with a mixture of sardonic pride and diffidence:

> A coward dies a thousand deaths.
> Rate me no coward then: 990-some yet to go.
> Just seven as I make it, three times with pneumonia
> (out of ten in all). Once Naples to Algiers
> flying the deck—that hungry waterspout.
> The kiefed-up sidi with the razor in the tram.
> Once coming out of anesthesia with
> an oxygen mask and much undue ado.
> Then this last time, so close they thought it best
> to take the copyright in my wife's name.

Of these eventful moments, the "Naples to Algiers" flight hugging the surface of the Mediterranean is, as I've already mentioned, used elsewhere in *Maximum Security Ward*, and the tram incident also belongs to Guthrie's months in Algiers trying to establish liaison with the French Resistance. (These were thoroughly unsatisfactory from his point of view, but he did manage to be one of the first Americans back in Paris after the Liberation, according to André Thirion in *Revolutionnaires Sans Revolution*.) This poem was written after the 1966–1967 draft, as is obvious from the reference to the copyright of *Asbestos Phoenix*—an extremely low-key way of summarizing a great deal of discomfort and danger accompanying Guthrie's therapy. The intensity of the cobalt treatments, for example, led to unexpected hemorrhaging and hospitalization in Paris in 1969, his last trip abroad—see "The Dutch Head Nurse"—and seriously jeopardized his ability to perfect *Maximum Security Ward*.[2] And of course the reference to surgery and oxygen mask fits in perfectly with the *Maximum Security Ward* ambience and particularly with the next two poems, which considerably disrupt the reminiscent vein that is not reestablished until we reach the fifteenth poem, "Fiercer Than Evening Wolves." Then it is put to the service of the vision of horror that dominates the last poems in part 1.

*   *   *

Between "'Side by Side'" and "Fiercer Than Evening Wolves" are six poems in as many different moods: "The Cube as a Wilted Prism," "Polar Bear," "The Archangel Michael," "Inventory," "The Flute," and "Icarus Agonistes." The peculiar flexibility of the sequence as a genre is at work here, for each of these poems is related to the others not so much logically as organically. That is, each contributes to the unfolding, under the psychological and physical pressures so obvious from the start, of a highly complex state of awareness. Each poem grows from preceding poems and prepares us for poems to come, but there is a certain openness in the process. Thus, although the actual order makes considerable aesthetic sense, it is not so absolutely rigid that the poems could not, perhaps, have been mixed in a slightly different way—or even have been moved to a position later in the sequence and other

2. Alexander Laing, Guthrie's close friend and literary executor, has recorded the struggle to finish *Maximum Security Ward* in "Pain, Memory and Glory: The Poetry of Ramon Guthrie."

poems substituted. At one time, for example, "The Flute" was near the end of *Maximum Security Ward*. Moved forward to its final position, it somewhat mysteriously telegraphs, rather than reiterates, the shift toward psychological equilibrium that occurs in part 2.

The first of the six poems, "The Cube as a Wilted Prism," picks up especially from "Today Is Friday." But it fuses the desperate immediacy of the earlier poem with a more aesthetically oriented perspective, echoing Giacometti's words in "Montparnasse" ("Sculpture anti-form—*of*, not *in*, space"):

> This cube
> has 6 faces, 12 edges, 24 angles
> each more fluctuating pinched and forced a-spread
> than all the others. Space. Sculpture not *in*
> but *of* space.

Also, the more analytical tone of "'Side by Side'" ("No fellowship . . . How the dying wince / from the living's shadows!") recurs as well:

> You might scream now if you so wished:
> sound cannot travel in such vast whiteness.
>
> Equation with death—liquescent crystal Death,
> as dry, invisible as pure
> self-consuming flame,
> becomes inevitable.
>
> The cross-hair sight of Never and Now
> is set in all zeniths, on all horizons.
> It is stamped with hot wire
> on my breastbone.

The images Guthrie chooses for the pressure of death (a drop forge that "chumbles and crunks more diamonds faster into dust," a cube that "contracting, shrinks tight within, upon itself— / soundless explosion squeezed to utmost condensation") culminate here in the "cross-hair sight," an image suggested in the "crisscross false horizons" of the first stanza. That this is the image Guthrie chooses as the equation of his own death suggests, I think, his inability to forgive himself for using such cross-hair sights on World War I bombing raids to deal death to others. Although the degree of destruction cannot compare with that of Vietnam—see the "thousand tons of bombs" in "'Loin de Moi'"—the remorse is so potent that it informs even the final poem of the sequence, "High Abyss," in which whatever salvation we can know is described in terms of a "dawn beyond all limit of horizon." If this reading is accurate, then the isolation attendant on such self-castigation carries over somewhat to the next poem, "Polar Bear."

Essentially, however, "Polar Bear" deals with a different kind of loneliness. The agitated patient of "Via Crucis," who is "no kith, belike, / or kin of anything—at least among the higher primates," here finds his psychological embodiment in the touching absurdity of a polar bear "that couldn't write poetry." This poem, one of the loveliest in *Maximum Security Ward*, also has a hospital setting, but from an earlier time when helplessness was met with kindness—in the form of a "small deft nurse" with copper-colored hair and bearing forgetfulness ("an easy needle slipped into my shoulder")—rather than with Mr. Goldblatt's ghoulish insensitivity. However, it is the dream image of the disoriented polar bear that dominates the poem:

> A polar bear who could not . . .
> Rocking his baffled muzzle to and fro
> groping for the tempo of a world
> empty of both sense and sound.
>
> I wondered—whatever was in the needle
> taking now effect—what had become of him
> and brooded over not trying to find a way to help him,
> staying at least to share
> the anguish of his white bewilderment.

The dream perspective allows an eerie shifting back and forth between the helpless, hopelessly incommunicado bear and the concerned but equally helpless poet, obviously two facets of the same personality.

The eleventh poem, "The Archangel Michael, or a reasonable facsimile thereof, holds a press conference"—based in part on Guthrie's schoolboy memories of a revivalist heard at Mount Hermon—deals with another kind of helplessness. The poem is a lively antiwar manifesto, linking political and evangelical rhetoric to the herd instinct that causes holy, and wholly murderous, crusades against the innocent:

> The press conference ends when the sergeants-at-arms,
> preceded by a huge bass drum, march in singing,
> *"Onward Christian soldiers, marching as to war,"*
> and carrying pikes on which heathen heads with
> wispy beards are impaled.

The irrationality of a Christian *soldier* or a Salvation *army* has struck many a concerned human being, and Guthrie takes particular pleasure in *Maximum Security Ward* in pointing up the differences between what could be considered a true Christian brotherhood and the kind of murderous one that actually seems to prevail in the twentieth century. (His brotherhood, we shall find, is made up of those more in touch with a true religious spirit, although they turn out to be quite oddly assorted.) In fact, the effect of self-righteous actions, whether chauvinistically or religiously motivated, is indirectly summarized in the opening lines of the next poem, "Inventory":

> Hmm, let's see now . . .
> On the left we have what is left
> On the right is what is right
> It is that simple . . .

Funny, of course, but there is a serious undercurrent: what is "left" after we have finished doing in the opposition is not necessarily what is "right." Or, as the poem puts it a few stanzas later: "On the left is nothing left / On the right nothing is right"—which acts as well as an epigrammatic comment on the political situation and the loss of true democratic and socialist values.

With "Inventory" the sequence draws breath for a moment and literally takes inventory of what has gone before, as well as providing lots of leeway for Guthrie's bawdily fertile imagination. Also, one of the best moments in *Max-*

imum Security Ward comes in the second stanza, when the old man figures out how to cope with the Mr. Goldblatts and their ginger ale, the ambience of the ward as a whole, and his own unacknowledged fears of what his diagnosis will be:

> To be a model patient you lie on your back,
> screen your eyes with the back of your wrist
> against the glaring cone of light
> and wait the chance to pour unnoticed
> the ginger ale into the urinal—
> bringing variety into the life
> of some laboratory technician.

The bawdy vein starts with the parodic "Faith, hope and clarity" ("I knew a girl named Faith once, / on shipboard and in both senses") and culminates in the images of the plural-breasted Diana of Ephesus and of Guthrie's chosen persona, Marsyas:

> Priapic Marsyas or Silenus as shown
> on a black-figured vase ("young man from Nantucket")
> tootling his heart out
> on upraised double flute . . .

Slyly related to the well-endowed young man of one of our raunchier limericks, Marsyas appears here at his most satyric. (One of the poems in *Asbestos Phoenix*, "The Poet to His Mind," asks for "an acute case of chronic priapism.") Marsyas, however, is not all lust; he is also "tootling his heart out," his double nature as satyr and artist conveyed by the visually similar, and reciprocally raised, phallus and flute.

That all this gaiety represents a desperate effort to counter loss of morale comes through in the closing stanza's prayer to the gamut of goddesses, its make-up somewhat changed from the sixth poem:

> Gamut of goddesses, Nerthus, Frigg (Friday's girl),
> Rosmertha and You
> the veiled and nameless one, bless me.
> Still the blood-flow in my veins,
> numb fingers' touch, quell thought and feeling

40

in my brain.
        For now,
surveying that churned wake, I know
that by some slip or quirk,
I have led a stranger's life, known with his mind,
spoken with his tongue, kissed with his lips,
worshipped or denied his gods . . .
    (Mix-up in cloak-room checks—
            sole-print perhaps)
and now must die this death of his for him.

Even here, in the midst of an appalled realization of just
how poorly one's life has lived up to expectations, the poem's
humorous vein is not entirely dropped. The swapped ba-
bies of the parenthetical allusion, of course immortalized
by Oscar Wilde in *The Importance of Being Ernest*, here serve
as a comic turn on the book's Ishmael motif. Still, the hor-
ror at imminent death after a life so thoroughly unsatisfac-
tory that it seems to have been led by a stranger is strik-
ingly conveyed, especially in the bitterly calm closing line:
"and now must die this death of his for him." This psycho-
logical splitting apart echoes the plight of patient and dream
polar bear, two poems back, "groping for the tempo of a
world / empty of both sense and sound." And the prayer
to "quell thought and feeling" is a more drastic turn on the
momentary forgetfulness that the "easy needle" supplied.
This particular state of mind, which showed up as "I have
always hated living" in the first poem and as "Let me be
never born" in the sixth, will be reinforced strongly in the
fourteenth poem, "Icarus Agonistes." Intervening, how-
ever, is a poem that picks up directly from the image of
Marsyas on the Greek vase.

In the 1966–1967 draft, "The Flute" served as a coda to
"'And the Evening and the Morning'" (which preceded
"The Red Virgin"). I only mention this because in the orig-
inal configuration the stage directions were not in the least
surprising: "MARSYAS: (*He takes his flute and seems about to
play it, thinks better of it and slips it back into the pocket of his
bathrobe. He resumes his meditation.*)" The impact of the poem
is considerably greater in the final arrangement; it seems

to rise out of unconscious depths as an intimation of a future in which the achievements of the great artists make life bearable:

> 'A stranger's life'? I said. *Many* strangers.
> Known with their minds . . . their eyes . . . their lips . . .
> Worshipped their gods . . . heard with their ears?
> Felt, have I, with their hearts—a moment mine?

Invoking negative capability again, we must wait for the twenty-fifth poem, "Caduceus," the forty-fifth, "'Visse, Scrisse, Amò,'" and the last, "High Abyss," before the positive implications of living a stranger's life—as opposed to the horror the conception conveys in "Inventory"—are fully understood. This intimation of the future is paralleled by the attempt of a figure from ancient mythology to play Mozart's String Quintet in G Minor (K. 516) on a flute. Naturally, we are not really dealing with an anachronism; "Marsyas" and "Mozart," double flutes and string quintets, are, as always, ways of embodyng states of mind and modes of artistic achievement that have endured from mankind's beginnings. Here, as in "Arnaut Daniel," a sense of personal failure fuses with humble respect for the enduring achievements of great artists. And, if Marsyas's disgust with his own ineptitude leads him to break his flute, he is also willing to accept the pieces back from friendly hands—a recognition, perhaps, that there is no shame attached to failure when one is up against overwhelming superiority. In fact, the fourteenth poem, "Icarus Agonistes," directly tackles the problem of taking on more than one possibly can, with the predictable results:

> The winnuh
>   and still champeen
>   is whatever
>   I got myself overmatched with
>   from the start.

This poem, like "Inventory," is closely connected with preceding poems. The "damsel with a clip-board" in the first stanza is out of Coleridge's "Kubla Khan" by way of Guthrie's "Via Crucis"; and the "ol' sport" is now almost a refrain, picked up from "Via Crucis" and "Inventory," carrying with it both the uneasy sense of isolation (sport in the biological sense) and the combative reaction Mr. Goldblatt's ministrations engendered. Actually, the title combines both: Icarus, as a flying man, was certainly a sport; and *agonistes* fits the patient's dream in "Via Crucis" of vaulting the side rail and ramming "those outsized, clicking dentures" down Goldblatt's throat. The implied reference to *Samson Agonistes* is also relevant—Icarus and Marsyas, like Samson, perished in their attempts to push themselves beyond their limits.

Icarus, in fact, is not named in the body of the poem. But his misadventures are clearly indicated in the second stanza, in which his fall from the sky is heard only by "one straggling and on the whole / incurious sheep." Like Auden, in his "Musée des Beaux Arts," or Williams in his "Landscape with the Fall of Icarus," Guthrie is following Brueghel's *Icarus*—as we discover in the twenty-second poem, "Icarus to Eve." Guthrie, however, treats this archetypal example of hubristic human endeavor with his own brand of sardonic humor: the indifferent sheep, the shepherd "gawking but in the diametrically / wrong direction." The vignette based on Brueghel's picture is followed, too, by a stanza that conjures up an innocently childish or naively religious belief in miracles:

> Stand on a haystack and flap your arms.
> You see, you almost *did* fly! Someday
> try it from the corncrib roof. Or, Joshua—
> hold up your arm and, as watching your shadow
> you can clearly see, stop the sun for a split second.

Who, after all, hasn't wished for such suspensions of natural laws? Out of such a need comes the belief in an afterlife, with which Guthrie takes issue in "There Are Those" but only hints at here in his revisionary *"mourir* is / *partir* quite a lot."

In the closing sections of the poem Guthrie modernizes the prayers in previous poems for oblivion, casting the orderly—or whoever is bringing sleeping pills to eager patients—as "Mr. Good Humor Man" and "Mister Summer-time Saint Nick" (Santa Claus will reappear hideously a few poems further on). He also provides a splendid little monologue by trainer to second-rate boxer, which closes with the same fatal pie-in-the-sky optimism that allows children to believe they might fly off the corncrib roof with impunity:

> "Awright, baby. We get him nex' time maybe.
> Him or somebody else.
> > Plenty times already
> you been flattened almost as bad as this."

IV. Napalm Santa Clauses
or Christoi?

"Icarus Agonistes" opens with a question repeated from "Via Crucis":

> A damsel with a clip-board in an Intensive Care Ward
> once I saw
> in a white uniform and she was asking,
> "Sir, what is your religion?" with a pencil poised
> to check it off. I should have said Black Muslim,
> but I didn't think of it until a week later.

We remember from "Via Crucis" that the answer is "None," with a sardonic follow-up: "She marks the X at Protestant." In both passages, then, the question of religious belief is treated lightly, yet it is actually one of the most serious preoccupations of the sequence. The next poem, moreover, "Fiercer Than Evening Wolves," gives us a glimpse of one powerful reason underlying Guthrie's hostility to organized religion. For if he urgently courts oblivion in "Icarus Agonistes" to "lay the ghosts" of "Twink" (Charles Amsden), Stella Bowen, and Norman Fitts—companions from his early days in France—the real ghost that needs to be put to rest is an even more intimate one: his mother's. It is evidently the impossibility of coming to terms with her life and death, as portrayed in "Fiercer Than Evening Wolves," that has had a profound effect on his ability to believe in a just and merciful God:

> Evenings between
> cooking and doing the housework and getting back
> to sewing, she would read the Bible to me.
> Especially the Old Testament. I liked that best—
> even Jeremiah and Habakkuk . . . *Their horses swifter*
> *than leopards and fiercer than evening*
> *wolves . . .*

and Ezekiel with his cherubim on beryl monocycles.
She skipped the parts about Dinah's boy-friend
getting circumcised and the two Tamars
and the Lord making the Israelites
hamstring the horses and rip up
the bellies of pregnant ladies.
Yes, the Lord God fared very well by Her—
better than She did by him, by far.

There is a gentle suggestion, in the capitals of the last two lines of this passage, that Guthrie's mother belongs, too, in his gamut of goddesses—although she herself was "truly pious," believing "totally, always, absolutely and without / shading or limitation." For the author of *Maximum Security Ward* such belief is half-enviable, not least because there might "be relief in having a God to hate." This appears to be the state of mind to which his mother was brought in her midforties after "successive strokes / twisted her mouth awry, mangled her speech, / paralyzed the right side of her body," and drove her to suicide:

Swallowing a massive dose of potassium chlorate—
no, not the cyanide she'd begged me for—
in the charity ward of the New Haven Hospital.

The bitterness of this poem is directed also toward a society so totally dominated by greed and self-interest—whatever its hypocritical lipservice to religious ideals—that it can cheerfully accept the presence of desperate, grinding poverty in its midst. In 1938 Guthrie wrote a polemical long poem, "Instead of Abel," in which the forces of capitalism, organized religion, and fascism are arrayed against the pure spirits represented by Seth and his ragged companions. A few of its sections were later published individually, but the poem's main importance seems to be that it allowed Guthrie to get beyond a rhetorically determined framework of Good versus Evil. Thus the bitterness still shines through, as here, but it is not allowed to dominate the structure of *Maximum Security Ward* or to vitiate the power of individual poems.

"The Oracles," the sixteenth poem, is a distillation of his

mother's fate, and the anguished, slack-mouthed Pythoness obviously has close affinities with the mangled woman of the preceding poem. Past, present, and future are maddeningly horrible—and irredeemable by either mortals or seers. In contrast to this hideous vision, the next poem, "There Are Those," introduces two innocently happy true believers who lovingly and gaily plan to get Guthrie into heaven with them. The poem skirts the sentimental, but Paddy and Mim's sweetness of spirit is evidently a valid component in what Einstein called "true religiosity" (quoted admiringly in the forty-sixth poem, "'And the Evening and the Morning'"), and they will be remembered at the very end of the sequence in "High Abyss." "There Are Those" also restores Guthrie's more lightly sardonic vein, missing since "Inventory":

> There are those—with mine own eyes I've seen them,
> heard them with my own ears—
> who still contrive to believe in heaven,
> locus undisclosed, though rather up than down.
> (Quoting sound authority, "All men will arise
> with the same bodies they have now." Is that
> something to feel good about?)

The next two poems, "The Prayers" and "'Loin de Moi,'" are companion poems. At the end of part 1—leaving aside for the moment the short twentieth poem, which acts as coda—a great many of the concerns from earlier poems in the sequence reappear, along with some signs of the way part 2 will develop. The climactic stanza is the last one of "'Loin de Moi'":

> So now, at what by my watch, if they would give it back to
>   me,
> must be about seven-thirty,
> I will not ask anything of any so-and-soing body
> in the world . . .
>   Certainly
> never to be human . . . The HUMAN RACE!
> No, not even for the laughs. The race of
> napalm Santa Clauses!
> Sheep herded by glib lies that greed concocts,

47

he-harpies safely out of sight and sound
cheerily showering some thousand tons of bombs
on the innocent helpless to strike back,
pointless despoilers and defilers of what
might elsewise be a fairly pleasant world.

AND YET . . .

This is one of the most concentrated and memorable passages spawned by the Vietnam War, reawakening in us with deadly accuracy our memories of "napalm Santa Clauses." Yes, we were guilty of murderousness, fatuous self-delusion, and a high tolerance for hype. *Maximum Security Ward* does not allow us to forget what it means to sacrifice others for the sake of some self-servingly pompous image of the United States as arbiter, on an international scale, of human values. For the moment, the sequence reveals quite nakedly one of the main pressures—political self-disgust—that has brought it into being. Yet this passage works better than Guthrie's more blatantly anti–Vietnam War poems because it floats free of any one war and is firmly enmeshed in concretely personal distress:

I never wanted to be *me*, in this at least
I found, it seems, fulfillment. (Listen carefully, cat,
cock your head on one side and wrap your tail
about your paws. You stand as good a chance
of understanding this as any.) I cannot think
of anyone less me than I am. There should be
surcease in that. Everybody—the red-headed intern,
the old man making death-sounds in the corner crib,
the low-slung nurse winding up her nightly stint . . .
Even the CHIEF HEAD IMPERIAL MR GOLDBALLS: STAFF NURSE
is more like me than I am.

In one way or another, all the previous poems can be related to this stanza: the "stranger's life" of "Inventory" and "The Flute," for example; or the details of the ward provided in many other poems; or the distaste for living, present since the opening elegy, which is so closely bound up with a sense that some other, infinitely more powerful

48

being or force has controlled one's life from the start. (As Guthrie puts it in the "Elegy for Mélusine"—in reference to the funeral but not limited to this one event—"I'm only playing the lead / in this production, not directing it.") This rich recapitulation of motifs is charcteristic of "The Prayers" as well as "'Loin de Moi'"; both poems, however, extend the range of the sequence in a number of interesting ways.

"The Prayers" starts straightforwardly enough, with the inquisitive young Ramon mulling over the efficacy of prayer. But at the opening of the second stanza the nature of prayer changes from request ("why not . . . ask for a hundred or a billion dollars") to question:

> Interrogatory prayer, whom are you asking what?
> "I'm asking the dead what death is like and the living
> what it is like to live. I am asking this housefly,
> sealed somehow between panes, perhaps hatched there,
> buzzing its life away against impenetrable light,
> whether it would rather be let out into
> the foreign air, stay where it is, or be
> let in and whacked by a flyswatter."

Guthrie's housefly "buzzing its life away against impenetrable light" is as attention catching as Emily Dickinson's ("I heard a Fly buzz—when I died"), and the subsequent peroration is a masterpiece of kindly lunacy ("Don't you want to copulate and eat and see / something of the world?") and informational overkill, as Guthrie bolsters his argument that "nothing was ever meant to live in houses" with examples drawn from the habits of the bedbug, allusions to relevant passages in *Faust* and the Bible, and a quick sketch of Louise Michel's (the "red virgin") ardent defense of liberty. Ishmael, Marsyas, and Abraham's ram also turn up briefly, reminding us of the patient's distraught state earlier in the sequence, and then the poem explicitly recalls the hospital:

> I am asking questions of the walls and ceiling,
> of the cocoon of bandages in a coma beside me.

I am asking questions of the ground and sky
of places I shall never see again.

There is a direct link here to *Pisan Cantos*: "we will see
those old roads again, question, / possibly / but nothing
appears much less likely" (Canto 74). Neither Guthrie nor
Pound lingers too long on the pathetic note however.
Guthrie moves on to Paddy and Mim and a slightly sala-
cious interlude with a "handsome Black Muslim mas-
seuse" and then to the kind of questions suggested by the
phrase "what it is like to live." Interrogatory prayer, then,
is not too different from the kind of curiosity that drives
scientists to find out all they can about the nature of things,
a dimension strongly suggested in the third stanza when
Guthrie, in the course of convincing the fly to "get the hell
outdoors," reminds it of the bedbug's scientific name.

Then, with a bit of help from the short prose passage
joining the outcast Ishmael to the unfortunate satyr, the
nature of prayer changes yet again:

> Exploratory prayer, addressed to whom?
> what are you asking It or Her or Him
> to say or do? What language, spoken by what
> paralyzed or petrified tongue, are you uttered in?
>
> Formed not of dust but quicksand.
> Lie prostrate in the muck, face buried deep in it,
> and try
> for breath to
> propitiate
> Him, Her, or It
> with gasping mad doxologies and screamed hosannahs.
>   . . . and yet
> . . . and yet
>   . . . ram caught by the horns
>   in a thicket. We find the theme
>   in gold and lapis lazuli at Ur of the Chaldees.
>   Poor bloody Marsyas—teach him to steer clear
>   of angels
> ("A little lower than the angels" . . . ,
> Some of whom
>   could walk under a snake's ass
> with high hats on . . . unquote the sergeant

who had served in the calvary
with Captain Black-Jack Perishing
christianizing them Moros in the Philippines)
and yet
        . . . And yet . . .

The conception of "exploratory" prayer suggests the search for the nature of divinity, and the passage brings out clearly the enduring presence of belief in the supernatural, in every culture and every time. It also suggests strongly that there is a very close relationship between the imagined nature of a supernatural being and the nature of the human beings doing the imagining: a violent and powerful god in need of constant propitiation to complement a race that finds the forceful subduing of weaker cultures in the name of religion quite natural. The modification of *Pershing* into *Perishing* and *cavalry* to *calvary* speak for themselves. This type of "christianizing" echoes the closing scene of "The Archangel Michael," with "Christian soldiers" carrying "pikes on which heathen heads with / wispy beards are impaled"; the echoes are heard again in the eleventh section of "Masque for Luis Buñuel," as Franciscan missionaries transfix small cannibals with gilded bows and arrows. And the panting, breathless attempts at propitiation will be explored at more leisure in the sacrifice of the "youths and girls" in "Apocalypse"—in which the Colossus destroying all civilization is cast in the image of nuclear holocaust.

The personal correlative to this disturbing intermingling of the religious spirit and violence is presented in "'Loin de Moi.'" The title—"far from me"—is borrowed from a poem by Robert Desnos. (Desnos moves through *Maximum Security Ward* as the archetypal poet, forced beyond himself by another holocaust, that of World War II—and whose greatest works of art, in the tradition of Guthrie's less publicly successful christoi, were inadvertently destroyed.) The poem opens with four of the most lyrical lines in the sequence:

Far from me
light shattering copper balls across

> the stubbled hillsides in October
> seeing fox pounce daintily on crickets.

Such moments are rare indeed in the sequence; they are the touchstones for the world of sanity and beauty and gentleness to which the maximum security ward and all forms of human violence are the antithesis. Other examples include the "brambled upland meadows" of "Scene: A Bedside in the Witches' Kitchen"; the lines about the flowerlike, copperhaired nurse of "Polar Bear"; the pastoral scene in "Caduceus"; the "willows budding" lines of "Arnaut Daniel"; scattered passages in "'Visse, Scrisse, Amò'"; a few lines in the fifth stanza of "Judgment Day"; and the description of the playful bear in "The Making of the Bear."

In the rest of the long section that opens "'Loin de Moi,'" Guthrie strips himself of all "honors, loves, and worships," ending with a prayer to the god who forsook Jesus on the cross to "let my self itself be far from me." This desire for self-dislocation echoes a number of the preceding poems and prepares us for the sixth stanza (quoted earlier: "I never wanted to be *me* . . . "). Most immediately, however, it relates to the exceedingly unpleasant conditions of the ward and to the poet's frantic realization that he may never get out of it sane or alive, never be able to make his own kind of harmony again:

> Far from me. Far from me. There is no return from here
> to color, clarity, or form. Sound aplenty
> but not a thud or scrape or drone to shape to any harmony.
> There is a stocky, squat, somebody's sister—
> somebody's daughter, at any rate—with swollen ankles,
> blouse like saddlebags. Night built up in layers
> of chlorine and last year's puke and piss.
> If I should beat my head against the bars,
> they would put it down to delirium.

The poem is one long crescendo to the closing "napalm Santa Clauses" stanza, touching on the other horrors of the ward, on Mélusine's desertion, on the vision of flaming planes carrying his friends to death in World War I, and on his own fall from the sky ("after the Sopwith fell apart"); indicting the whole "human world," especially "these United States" as a death house; recalling the distraught frame of mind of the opening "Elegy" ("sizzle out like crackerbarrelers' spit"); and in general knotting together a great many of the strands of the sequence. The closing line, "AND YET . . ." —also at the end of the preceding poem—points ahead to the second part. More immediately, however, it suggests that we should read the next poem, "Boul' Miche, May 1968," with dual vision. This closing poem of part 1 is more than an indictment of police brutality at the time of the students' and workers' riots in Paris. It also celebrates the heroism of the brave young man, not directly involved, who steps into danger anyway:

> Not only had never seen the girl before   was not a
> student nor even a sympathizer. On the whole against
> the lot of them for burning cars and felling all those
> trees for barricades   But when cops took to clubbing
> girls for fun . . .

And the last stanza, picking up on one of the narrow escapes from death mentioned in "'Side by Side,'" also points to all the brave, uncelebrated, daring human beings who in part 2 will swell the ranks of the christoi:

> (Thunderclaps are heard.
> Off Scylla a waterspout scours seashells
> from the seabed and hurls them above the clouds.
> The young English pilot tugs the wheel
> and hauls the yoke into his gut.)

*   *   *

The first stanza of "Don't and Never Did," the opening poem in part 2, excerpts the fifth of "'Loin de Moi,'" which reads in its entirety:

> (I never asked to be human. I don't and never did
> opt to be human. Given any choice, I should rather
> have been begotten by a dog-fox on a vixen
> or an alley tom on a good mouser or—
> though that may be too much to wish—

not to have been begotten at all. Quarter of a billion
spermatozoa scatter-sprayed, one gets its random target,
to the ultimate consternation of all concerned.

The retraction offered in "Don't and Never Did" is based
on the presence of "certain humans" beside whom one is
privileged to stand, "even from afar." Neither immortality
nor insentience (Zeus or a grain of sand) matches this priv-
ilege. Even on the brink of death,

my choice would stay the same.
                              I say this knowing
that soon in some brash, noisome realm
where Pluto-Goldblatts reign, and weary, hurrying,
taut or soggy nurses are all there are
in line of houris, I shall die—
last installment on the price of being man.

The poem recalls both "Via Crucis" and "Elegy for "Mélu-
sine.""A splendidly lively attack on Mr. Goldblatt at last
puts the water-and-ginger-ale episode to rest:

Aroint! I said. Scuttle back crabwise
into that foul funnel of your web,
drawing that musty effluvium of yours behind you.
Yes, I still want a drink but not that badly.
Better men than ever I was have died of thirst.

And the brash funeral of the "Elegy" is replaced by a much
humbler version:

Don't shave and rouge and powder me,
slick down my hair. Don't make me look presentable,
which I never did except young and naked
or all decked out in battle dress with all the ribbons.
Let me look dead and tired and old,
and no one look on me.

   These shifts in perspective continue into the next poem,
"Icarus to Eve," in which failure is humorously counterbal-
anced by the importance of the attempt:

Madam, I am Icarus, your son.
Wax melted when I flew too near . . . Remember?
No? There's no wonder. I have so many siblings

that the only wonder is that even
an absent-minded sheep should note our fall.

> (Without us, legs would still be fins.
> "Johnny! Don't you go too near that land.
> You want to get all dry!")

Then, in the twenty-third poem, "This Stealth," the quintessential human quality is spelled out:

> Human I never would have chosen to be,
> yet grant the poor bastard this: his lust, unlost
> for all frustration, to push his way beyond
> whatever he is.

This explicit statement is dropped into the midst of a poem that conjures up prehistoric aeons, working backward from the cave painters (one of whom is recreated so splendidly in "The Making of the Bear") to the dawn of humanity:

> At what point something ceased
> being whatever it was and became
>   human—
> first animal aware
> of death—not even the most assiduous
> study of a stray molar here and there
> will let us say.

The next poem, "The Christoi," takes us out of myth and prehistory into the modern world. Its reliance on vignettes of human beings who have brought back "secrets for changing life" (Guthrie is quoting Rimbaud) signals a major shift in the dynamics of the sequence. From now on, the portraits of especially admirable human beings make for a looser and more expansive structure. However, the private agonies of these beings, which serve as stark reminders of Guthrie's own condition, as well as his continued aesthetic control, keep the sequence from sputtering out under a welter of descriptive material.

The derivation of the words *christos* and *christoi*—which, Guthrie tells us, rhyme respectively with *lees toss* and *lees toy*—is self-evident: from the Greek word for *anoint* by way of Christ to a secular pantheon:

> Anointed, elect, chosen.
> Chosen by whom?
> Why, by themselves, I think.
> Settle for christos, christoi.
>
> Yes, *they* did the choosing. Chose once for all
> and then again at every moment. Wisdom learned
> at every choice making the next choice harder—
> and easier!

To be a christos, one must be both hero (or heroine) and saint, and Guthrie finds these qualities in quite a varied list. For a start, he nominates Prometheus ("except for being / slightly more mythical perhaps than some"), who chose eternal torture rather than "prolong gods' tyranny over man"; the great painters (we should remember that Guthrie was himself a fine amateur painter) from cave artists to Rembrandt; and musicians and composers from the inventor of the flute to J. S. Bach.

> The need is for a word to cover all
> who try to scale the face of heaven, thieves of fire,
> to bring back "secrets for changing life,"
> every Prometheus, from the Aurignacian
> who gouged mammoths in the cave of Arcy
> to the man of Amsterdam who painted
> the flayed ox carcass, from the one who first
> pierced holes in reeds to him who died known mostly
> as the sire of twenty children and highly skilled
> performer on both organ and clavichord.
> (The *great* Bach, most agreed
> was Karl Philipp Emanuel.)

Note how suggestive the passage is within the context of *Maximum Security Ward*: Marsyas, like Prometheus, challenged a god and was tortured for it, and in "Arnaut Daniel" he is associated, like Prometheus, with the struggle for human liberty; the subject of Rembrandt's *Flayed Ox* (alluded to again in "'And the Evening and the Morning'") is excruciatingly close to poor Marsyas, likewise hoofed; and the flute was, of course, Marsyas's instrument. Bach's lack of recognition in his own time is a familiar motif in the sequence, handled with particular effectiveness in "Arnaut Daniel."

Whom else does Guthrie nominate in "The Christoi" to be among his chosen people? Saint-Just, "age 26 years two days, / standing on the scaffold in his master's blood," is one. (In "'Visse, Scrisse, Amò'" Guthrie cites his contriving to get a Paris street named for the French revolutionary leader as his "greatest source of lasting satisfaction.") The "boy choosing prison rather than be sent / to murder freedom-lovers half a world away" is another. Reappearing, along with his "young wife," in "Judgment Day," he symbolizes all such resistance in any country and any time—rather more satisfactory than his identification in "Scherzo for a Dirge" in *Asbestos Phoenix* as a draft resister during the Vietnam War. Cézanne, "stopping to wash his brush after every stroke / to keep his mind a fresh blank for that choosing / less choice than discovery," is one. Proust, the great novelist whose *Remembrance of Things Past* Guthrie taught year after year and whose exalted view of art's ability to reveal one's true self and the innermost essence of life—see in particular *Time Regained*—Guthrie shared, is another. In the passage on Proust, which is laced with quotations from his work, *Maximum Security Ward* presses the highest claims for art. It is seen as springing out of the deepest religious impulses of man and as being vital to discovering and essentially making one's self (of some importance, naturally, to one who feels he has led a "stranger's life" and cannot think of "anyone less me than I am"):

> Every choice
> a choosing (discovering) of self and selves
> to *make* the choice. *"Un des moi . . . l'autre moi . . .*
> *le moi qui venait de renaître . . . "* (Unless
> ye be born again . . .)
> The pampered little pederast chose nameless God
> and, choosing God, chose agony and abnegation,
> perpetual adoration.
> Devoured by the cancer of holy Joy, the blessèd
>   anguish . . .
> *cet appel vers une Joie supra-terrestre"*

(the *appel* itself is Joy). Consumed,
eaten away, by "ineffable Joy . . ."

The catalog continues. Gabriel Péri, "facing the firing
squad at Mont-Valérien" is a christos. A member of the
French Resistance and a Communist, he is hauntingly de-
scribed in "Desnos" as dying "pour des lendemains / qui
chantent." (In "Dead: How to Become It," from *Graffiti*,
having one's blood "drilled . . . into the prison wall of Mont-
Valérien" is, along with other instances of courage and
sacrifice during World War II, one of the great ways to die.)
Also christoi, although "not entirely housebroken," are
Beethoven with his "unbearable" eating habits and other
social lapses, the criminal Villon, and the lice-infested Rim-
baud. Perhaps even Wallace Stevens makes the grade, and
certainly the "common" man who is uncommonly he-
roic does:

> Some of them are indeed Titans
> But I am struck by so many of them
> being ordinary men differing from their neighbors
> only by speaking out when others are keeping silent,
> by saying "No" when others are giving dull assent,
> by looking at situations clearly
> and acting, within their means, accordingly,
> by branding lies as lies.
> What did he mean (this insurance executive) by
> "The common man is the common hero?"

This passage leads into the striking hieroglyphic poem
"Caduceus," which intertwines Guthrie, Stevens, and
Rimbaud (seasoned with a dash of Whitman and Williams)
with a success undreamed of by Herbert or other seven-
teenth-century experimenters with pattern poetry. Guth-
rie's symbol of healing boasts a staff that scatalogically con-
verts the title of Stevens's "Thirteen Ways of Looking at a
Blackbird" into an emblem of poetry written under more
immediately pressing circumstances: *There are at least 19
ways of being shat on by as many different kinds of black birds.*
The snakes or ribbons that twine around the staff of the
caduceus picture the poet at Whitmanic ease, "lying on his

/ belly by the towpath, / heels crossed above his back," as "new and lush" as the meadow grass in which he is lying. This is "sprinkled," in a way Williams would have appreciated, with "pale / flowerets too frail and insignificant / to have a name." Rimbaud's pronouncement in a letter to Paul Demeney that "I" is "another," is converted here into "beaucoup d'autres"—the many others that surfaced mysteriously in "The Flute" ("'A stranger's life?' I said. *Many* strangers") and will play an important role in "'Visse, Scrisse, Amò.'" ("We have lived strangers' lives / in depths and breadths of worlds they lived / and died to make.") And the last line—"Il n'y avait donc pas de merles en Abyssinie?"—provides a fantastic explanation for Rimbaud's abandoning poetry at a young age: no black birds in Abyssinia to cause the proper trouble. (There may also be a slight allusion here to Coleridge's Abyssinian maid, who has already turned up in "Icarus Agonistes" as a "damsel with a clip-board.")

After this extraordinary interlude, the sequence returns to a more traditional vein with "Desnos," a companion poem to "The Christoi." Guthrie piles up more examples of those elect who "bear witness, / some in a warped, obscure, circumvented way, / to human dignity." Robert Desnos—"once his life and words caught flame" in the holocaust of World War II—"stands among the christoi." (Desnos will be hailed again in the thirty-eighth poem, "Not Dawn Yet.") Also present are Péri, van Gogh, Balzac, Mozart (despite his enthusiasm for "dreck"—dung), the sculptor of the Venus of Lespugue, and Giacometti:

> Christoi all
> those whose little donkey-rides
> are preludes to Golgothas.

These humbler versions of Christ are often bumblingly inept and driven, so that an epitaph for a typical christos might read:

> "HERE lies buried an unknown chosen one
> marked mostly
> for his various ineptitudes.

> That glow about his head, sometimes mistaken
> for a halo,
> was the buzzing contrail of the Furies."

Desnos, however, died "all poet and hero and all saint," his heart beating "for Liberty / to the very rhythm of the seasons and the tides / of day and night." Yet he was also a common man, who just happened to be caught up in the concentration camp nightmare of the war: "And, being human, would not allow being made / a walking carrion to diminish his humanity." Running through all the portraits of the christoi is this gentle insistence on common humanity: the common man is indeed the "common hero."

V. "Descended into hell"

From the twenty-seventh poem ("And It Came to Pass") on, portraits of christoi punctuate the momentum of the sequence. These work quite well on the whole; they are both lively and in one way or another urgent. Hovering over "And It Came to Pass," for example, is the question of what Luther Burbank actually accomplished:

> "Wizard of Plants!" the obituaries screamed.
> "Never in all the history of horticulture . . .
> Eight-hundred-odd creations . . . The mind reels
> to think . . . One of the greatest
> benefactors . . . "
>
> The facts . . . Well, he did develop and name
> the Shasta Daisy—"handsome in borders . . .
> soon dies out . . . best grown as a biennial."
> Most of the other things—pitless prunes, plumcots,
> white blackberries—seem not to have caught on,
> though, where it has not reverted, jackrabbits
> will eat spineless cactus for want of other food.

In the thirtieth poem, "Black Squirrels and Albert Einstein," the essential isolation of one human being from another cuts through the vignettes of poet and "Mado, wondrous little whore girl," and of Einstein attempting to carry on a conversation with his neighbor:

> "All he could talk about was squirrels. No kiddin'—
> black squirrels with tufted ears!
> Seems in the old country that's how they come."

In "Yorick," the portrait of a stifled painter—recalling the bone-chilling ambience of the "polar bear that couldn't write poetry"—is sharpened by the presence of a far more easy-going, successful artist, Paul Burlin, "who at that time was painting / lopsided incandescent cows erupting / into explosive heavens." Meanwhile, poor, desperate Yorick is surrounded by

Stillborn canvases stacked against the walls,
ready to be turned face-out and shown
if ever anybody cared to see them.
Seven viae dolorosae to the week
and every night Gethsemane.

"Yorick a christos? Who's to say?" the poem ends. The hero of the thirty-second poem, "Masque for Luis Buñuel," could surely find his halo intact—except that the "murky radiance of his hallucinatory world" has been appalling enough to drive him to an alcoholism that destroys his art. In the thirty-sixth poem Georges Guynemer, the World War I ace, loses his luck and simply vanishes. In the next poem Hemingway blows his brains out, Desnos dies "the more the saint and hero for having few illusions," and his fabulous companion Youki ("who had made history / of a kind in Tokyo by going as Eve / to a diplomatic *ballo in maschera*") ends up drunk and dead. Desnos's death is treated more extensively in the thirty-eighth poem, "Not Dawn Yet," in which an essential distinction is made:

Having this prickly twig a kindly fighting-girl
had given him was good. Having lived through
to liberty was good. Being a poet,
being a man was good.
Did that mean life was good? Had been? Is?
Allons, mon p'tit! Non, mais tu veux rire!
But being human, yes, at times . . . at times
when men are human.

No, I would not secede.
Not for all the Himmlers, Johnsons, Quislings,
Calvins, Torquemadas. I would not secede
even if I could be a grain of sand,
sovereign and absolute.

The "I" who would not secede is Guthrie, inspired by Desnos, Einstein, Beethoven, Sisley, Blake, Chardin, Giotto, Williams, Villon, Stendhal, El Greco, Ravel:

All of them . . .
Yes, the Yoricks, the gaunt, undaunted Yoricks.
All the race of blundering doers and undoers

of their destinies, the fumblers, the tanglers of their skeins,
the Masters, whose common anguishes we,
dazzled by their glories (invisible to them),
cannot see.

These "invisible" glories certainly inform "Arnaut Daniel," "Anabasis" with its cuckolded scholar and poor guitarist, and "The Red Virgin," in which Louise Michel dies "possessed of a few trinkets and piles / of manuscript." Her funeral procession, however, "took nine hours to pass." And if the cave painter of the penultimate poem, "The Making of the Bear," works with no hope at all of his bear ever being seen ("but he still is there"), the sequence brings the painting to life again, just as the caves of Niaux and Lascaux and Altamira were brought to light many thousand years later.

We could linger over each of the portraits to the extent that we did with "Arnaut Daniel": they charm us and surprise us; they repossess the prehistorical in "The Making of the Bear," revivify the historical in "Arnaut Daniel" and "The Red Virgin," illuminate the contemporary in "And It Came to Pass," "Masque for Luis Buñuel," and "Black Squirrels and Albert Einstein," and resurrect the biographical in "Yorick" (modeled on a friend of Guthrie's, Myron Nutting), "Desnos," "The Dutch Head Nurse," "Death with Pants On," "For Approximately the Same Reason," and "Anabasis." (A comparison of "And It Came to Pass" with John Dos Passos's portrait of Burbank in *The 42nd Parallel* indicates just how well Guthrie works in this mode.) And they provide the touchstones for sanity as the sequence enters some of its darkest moments.

All along, *Maximum Security Ward* has worked on several levels. There is the immediate physical distress that has sent the old man to the intensive care unit in the first place, which is combined with a sickening sense of betrayal: at its simplest, the feeling—irrational or not—that no one really cares. Then there is the less personal, more communal realization that the human race, especially the members of it living in "these United States"and waging war in Vietnam, has betrayed its best possibilities. Exacerbating all this physical, personal, and social distress—to put it crudely—there is not only the terrible sense of imminent death but an equally terrible sense that one has run out of time both as a man and as an artist. The key questions here are whether one is good enough ("Nothing I have ever done . . . was worth the doing") and whether one has been granted enough time to have an impact on civilization. A comforting aspect of the portraits is that the christoi frequently do not realize the enduring quality of their art; or, just as long as they know they have created something marvellous, they are content, as is the maker of the bear, to have their achievement go unrecognized:

> Beside the profound, absolute
> dark of caves, our night seems noon.
> Even beneath a starless sky,
> the eye makes out bulk and shapes,
> but in winding scapes of underground
> where no sun's light has ever shone,
> finger may touch the lash
> of open eye unseen.
>
>   There
> in that total lack of light
> is where my bear is.
> No one will ever see him
> but he still
> is there.

But before we reach the cluster of poems closing *Maximum Security Ward*, in which life emerges tentatively as having been worth living, there are such poems as "Good Friday," "The Surf," "And the Veil of the Temple Was Rent," "By the Watch," and two poems of nuclear holocaust, "Apocalypse" and "The Brocken." These are intermingled with the portrait poems and, in any case, are not unrelievedly black—just as the portrait poems are not unrelievedly cheerful.

*   *   *

Part 2 can be somewhat arbitrarily divided into a group of eighteen poems from "Don't and Never Did" through

"Not Dawn Yet" and the closing group of eleven, from "Arnaut Daniel" through "High Abyss." "Not Dawn Yet" obviously completes the argument with the self started in "'Loin de Moi,'" partially resolved in "Don't and Never Did," as to whether one should have "opted to be human." And Guthrie's plunge into Arnaut's psyche in the next poem is the acting out of the way to health indicated in "Caduceus." His "I" has indeed become another; he has appropriated another world view, in essence lived a new life. Toward the end of the sequence the role of art in making possible this great expansion of the spirit is given more and more attention, especially in the five closing poems, "'Visse, Scrisse, Amò'" through "High Abyss."

Let us return for a moment to the beginning of part 2 and the first four poems: "Don't and Never Did," "Icarus to Eve," "This Stealth," and "The Christoi." By the closing lines of the fourth poem—"What did he mean (this insurance executive) by / 'The common man is the common hero?'"—the sequence has offered considerable support for the essentially irrational decision in "Don't and Never Did," to "choose / rather to be human, to stand beside / certain humans, even from afar." "Caduceus" then beautifully disrupts the meditative mode with its visual pattern and concretely suggestive imagery of intertwined artistic imaginations. If, as the poem suggests, the way to health will involve an ability to be many others (in fact, many different kinds of others), there will be dark sides to the experience—the blackbirds will be present in every realm of the imagination, even the most purely lyrical and beautiful. We immediately see this darkness at work in the horror of the next poem, "Desnos," with its description of the poet's brutal treatment at the hands of the Nazis. This description is balanced somewhat in the next poem, "And It Came to Pass," by the much lighter treatment of Luther Burbank and his detractors:

And it came to pass that the Lord God spoke out of
    the mouth
of a Kansas preacher and said unto Luther Burbank,
"If I had meant there to be pitless prunes,

> white blackberries, spineless cactus and blue poppies
> I would damn well have made them that way."

"And It Came to Pass" also has its dark moments, most notably the glancing blow at the Vietnam War in the third stanza ("back in 1941 when there were still / choo-choo cars and atoms were unsplit / and forcing young men to baste babes in napalm / from safe distances would have been considered in bad taste"). Also, however, there is the dilemma set up in the poem's opening stanza:

> . . . Not so much an anagogic urge
> as an impious itch to change
> himself, his world, his universe,
> without the slightest certainty of bettering them . . .

And there is that doubt, at the end of the poem, as to whether the world has really been much altered by Burbank's work, no matter how hysterically complimentary his obituaries were.

In the next two poems we move out of the historical realm occupied by Desnos and Burbank and into a hybrid of myth and history. Whereas before there was the mythical Icarus, now, in "Good Friday," the namesake of the christoi is introduced somewhat irreverently but no less seriously for that. Here, too, there is the possibility that even Christ did not know whether his existence changed the world and the universe for the better:

> I am trying to see the man's face.
> The answer is there, there and in what
> he is doing with his hands.
> Waving ackowledgment of cheers? Uplifted
> in benediction. Raised in a V sign or triumphant
> clenched fist? ("The winnuh and still
>   champeen . . . ")
> I cannot see the face.

The repeated phrase at the end of the poem, "Descended into hell" (flippantly qualified by references to modern ticker tape parades and Palm Sunday's borrowed donkey), leads directly to the personal descent into hell in

"The Surf." We should notice, incidentally, that Guthrie does not attempt a literal description of the crucifixion. It would, in fact, be superfluous in a work that has made such a point of linking individual suffering to that archetypal event. Similarly, "The Surf" sidesteps Christ's resurrection by referring in the second stanza to the other famous resurrection in the Christian tradition, that of Lazarus:

> This is the fourth day   and no coming forth . . .
>   Lazarus, you remember meeting me in hell?
> Marsyas, the name is.
> "No, I cannot say I do."
>   *I* remember   I remember
> I remember only the white
> surf roar and the dank spume
> of loneliness.

In conveying the quality of hell, "The Surf" concatenates a number of images associated with death that are used elsewhere in the sequence. Indeed, the opening words, "WHITE NOISE," recall the "white hollow roar" of the third poem, "Today Is Friday," and the "vast whiteness" that is an equation for "liquescent crystal Death" in "The Cube as a Wilted Prism." Furthermore, the phrase anticipates the description in the thirty-seventh poem, "For Approximately the Same Reason Why a Man Can't Marry His Widow's Sister," of Hemingway's body ("No longer apple-cheeked or cheeked at all. / One WHITE silent bang where head had been") as well as the "SHATTERING WHITE SILENCE" of "'And the Evening and the Morning.'" Also mentioned in the first stanza are the grain of sand, which has stood for the most inanimate of objects, and sheep, huddled "in the fog, / lost together," reminding us of all their other appearances in this book—the sacrificial ram, the sheep who watch (or fail to watch) the fall of Icarus, the sheep served up at dinner in "Masque for Luis Buñuel" ("'Feed my sheep.' / 'Yassir. To whom, Lord?'"), and so forth. At the end of the second stanza, the "deafening crump" that has "long been going on" actively recalls the death imagery of "Today Is Friday" and "The Cube as a

Wilted Prism." The names the protagonist takes for himself in the third stanza (Adam, Icarus, Marsyas, Ishmael, Merlin) bear with them disastrous connotations, and the cry to Mélusine from the "dank, jumbled death-bin" in the last stanza recalls all the death-fraught atmosphere of the intensive care unit.

Four poems along, after "Black Squirrels and Albert Einstein," "Yorick," "Masque for Luis Buñuel," and "The Dutch Head Nurse," we reach "And the Veil of the Temple Was Rent," whose title refers specifically to Christ's passion. Its final lines intertwine the artist's anguished outcry, "Nothing I have ever done . . . was worth the doing," with Christ's despairing words on the cross. The Christian frame of reference continues in the thirty-fifth poem, "By the Watch," when the unthinking, casual killing of a snake leads to what on the surface seems excessive remorse:

> The spring
> is spoiled for me, the summer, the garden
> that was to have been beautiful, the year
> and years to come.
> It was a young handsome thing of grace,
> exploring with its flickering tongue the world
> it was to live in. If I could be a moment Christ,
> my single miracle would heal and resurrect it.

"By the Watch" may not, in fact, avoid the sentimental—despite the more rigorous stanzas surrounding the episode in the garden. However, this very sentimentality gives it a special place in the dynamics of *Maximum Security Ward*. For the moment the language of the sequence is washed clean of anger, bitterness, and all signs of intense psychological struggle. Out of deep exhaustion and weakness, as it were, the "tears of things" come flooding in. There is a similarity, surely, to the momentary wavering that led the crucified Christ to cry out, "My God, my God, why hast Thou forsaken me?" Moreover, this snake obviously stands in for all the innocent people—especially children—who have been helplessly slaughtered throughout our history:

("Don't never die till sundown.") Come quickly, sundown.
Come quickly. I will stand beside it,
trying, by covering it with warm dust
as one lays one's coat over a hurt child in shock,
to ease its going.

The end of the poem contrasts this kind of killing with that of war, in which both parties have agreed to risk their lives to kill each other. "Death was a way that they and I had chosen," Guthrie says of the World War I fights in which he manned the De Havilland Four's machine gun:

Woke each morning expecting to be dead
by nightfall, not too much concerned about it.
    "Man, this here airman's feeling
pretty trepid. No special hunch or anything—
just feeling trepid."

The thirty-sixth poem, "Death with Pants On," is primarily a tribute to the "ace of aces," Guynemer, a hero who had chosen the "way" of death. Its last stanza, however, memorializes young men who had made no such choice but had simply been herded into a deadly situation:

                    I think of others
Chapin, Sayre, Comygies, Nick Carter
whom I last saw spinning down in flames
toward La Chaussée. Their first fight—
if you can call it that. Unmatched for unreality:
as we straggled out of clouds into a well
of open sky, the red-nosed hornets swooped.
Most of us
never found a chance to fire a shot.
There were others. I forget their names.

In "'Loin de Moi'" it was these young men Guthrie envied for having been allowed to die "with pants on," while he has aged and become effectively imprisoned behind his bed bars, "stifling in the rutty goat smell / of MR. GOLD-BLATT:STAFF NURSE and death." Two writers who died with pants on are Desnos and Hemingway, described in the next poem. Desnos knew what he risked when he chose to speak out on behalf of freedom fighters everywhere, and Hemingway took his own life. Why, Guthrie wonders, has he failed to take the same way out? One answer—"speak no ill of curiosity; / it has kept me living, lo, this many a year"—recalls the ebullient questions about life and living in "The Prayers." But the description of the "mean and hungry" waterspout on the flight from Naples to Algiers takes us back to "'Side by Side'" and the "living who do not want / even in their secret hearts to die." The instinct for survival obviously cannot be dismissed lightly:

> "God, this isn't praying. This is just to say
> I'd hate to die before I learn
> what happens to Mussolini."

This lightening of spirit ("how to choose the day when there would be / nothing to be curious about?") is reflected in the next poem, "Not Dawn Yet," in some slight shifts in the way the ward is perceived:

> Not dawn yet   or ever
> though the silence is no longer white and blank
>   and has somewhat abated
>   (The square-bottomed nurse says,
>   "Look, if those bars really bother you . . .
>   We aren't supposed to
>   but if I was just so busy I forgot . . . ")
> somewhat abated
>   Nor is the protracted CUBE as absolute
>   nor the click so irrevocable.

Then Desnos appears for the last time, having suffered through to the realization, as he dies, that although it is totally inappropriate to speak of "life" as "good,"

> Having this prickly twig a kindly fighting-girl
> had given him was good. Having lived through
> to liberty was good. Being a poet,
> being a man was good.

The poem ends with the firmest statement in *Maximum Security Ward* of reconciliation to one's own nature as a

member of the human race; and, significantly, this last cat-
alog of the christoi includes only writers, painters, and
composers: Beethoven, Sisley, Blake, Chardin, Giotto, Wil-
liam Carlos Williams, Villon, Stendhal ("Arrigo Beyle, Mil-
anese"), El Greco ("Domenico Theotocopuli"), and Ravel.
It is a shift in emphasis that leads us into the last poems of
the sequence.

*   *   *

The success of "Arnaut Daniel (circa 1190)" not only as
an individual poem but as one of the radiating centers of
Maximum Security Ward should be more obvious now than
it was earlier. The shift to the first person is crucial. This
christos springs to life with all his "vulnerabilities and ser-
vitudes" made tangible to our imaginations. Also, the in-
tertwining of Arnaut's voice with that of Marsyas at the
beginning and that of the modern poet at the end demon-
strates perfectly what it means to be "kin of the christoi, of
their race." It also suggests the joyous and painful dimen-
sions of what it means to live strangers' lives ("The Flute")
and to be many different kinds of others ("Caduceus").
Marsyas's casual reference to the Romans' setting up his
statue as a symbol of liberty resonates strongly in the wake
of the preceding references to sacrifices in the name of
liberty, in particular those of Desnos and Louise Michel.
(She was mentioned briefly in "The Prayers" and will reap-
pear as "The Red Virgin.")
   Arnaut's awareness of death and projection of how much
he will miss spring and the young girls is of a piece with
Guthrie's yearning for Mélusine and other times and places;
its lyricism recalls, too, the opening passage of "'Loin de
Moi,'" with the wistfully remembered "stubbled hillsides
in October." And the continued sexual interest echoes most
immediately "The Dutch Head Nurse" (the scene is the
American Hospital of Paris), with its description of the
"happy young Lapland nurse":

   "Is okay my coontry only is too much cold
   and winters is no sun. Is good only for reindeers."

71

>   She was no reindeer   rather a bright-eyed
>   flicker-tailed ibex or chamois
>   with nimble thighs that only fear of seeming senile
>   kept me from stroking.

I could go on—Arnaut's fear that his poems will not survive throws into relief the destruction of Desnos's best poems, the "not too unlovely world" in which Arnaut lived recalls the "fairly pleasant world" of "'Loin de Moi,'" and so forth. But I think it is clear enough that this thirty-ninth poem has the power to orient around itself all the preceding poems and to irradiate many of the poems to come as well.

The first of this final group, "Anabasis," presents abbreviated portraits of a scholar and a "Puerto Rican kid" as humble kin of the christoi. The next two poems are the holocaustical "Apocalypse" and "The Brocken." Then come the extended portraits of Louise Michel ("The Red Virgin") and of the common man as common hero ("People Walking"). In the eschatalogical trio of "'Visse, Scrisse, Amò,'" "'And the Evening and the Morning,'" and "Judgment Day," the experience of being human is judged for the last time. The forty-eighth and forty-ninth poems, "The Making of the Bear" and "High Abyss," are striking testimonials of Guthrie's belief that the creative artistic spirit is the essence of being human and at one with the true religious spirit.

The first section of "Anabasis" is a long echo back to the "Elegy for Mélusine from the Intensive Care Ward," in which the patient reflects on his future pallbearers' stopping dead in their tracks: "Their tracks to *where?* / Don't ask *me*: I'm only playing the lead / in this production, not directing it." The observation in "Anabasis" that "the more he rode, the farther he went" similarly suggests some confusion over the direction one's life is taking; indeed, all the people in the poem wonder why they are doing what they are. This bemused sensibility is linked to Guthrie both as patient (the conductor lurching down the aisle speaks in Goldblatt's idiom) and as scholar ("Foundations awarded him grants and wondered why"), but it could be that of any scholar, artist, or scientist understood neither by himself nor by others and whose work may or may not last. The aura of humble accomplishment is reinforced by the aspiring guitarist of the second section, whose playing is "pretty good considering that he didn't know how / to tune it, had never tried to play / any instrument before and had no ear for music anyway." That the Puerto Rican youth is of the same ilk, however, as Marsyas, Ishmael, and patient emerges in the last lines, given in his own language. The Spanish translates as "Ishmael? I am Marsyas, your blood brother. Do you remember me? Mélusine, do you remember me?"

"Apocalypse"—like "The Archangel Michael"—is in Guthrie's strongly satirical mode. Its expansive rhetoric suggests the style of some of the poems in *Graffiti*:

> All precautions have been taken:
> lampposts have been strung with garlands,
> wreaths hung about the necks of statues,
> certain graffiti that have of late appeared
> on the walls of public buildings been effaced
> and plainclothesmen posted to apprehend
> their skulking perpetrators.

Into the midst of the municipal festival and its criminally obtuse, fun-oriented, self-congratulatory mayor, councilmen, and citizens strides the colossus from "Fiercer Than Evening Wolves." He combines elements of violent god as well as Rhodian Colossus, and gullible mortals imagine that he might possibly be propitiated (more quietly, however, than with the "gasping mad doxologies and screamed hosannahs" of "The Prayers"):

> Do not cast flowers in his way: he does not care for flowers.
> Nor palm leaves: he does not care for palms.
> Only let our youths and girls—those carefully chosen,
> those only without blemish—cast themselves
> silently before Him, their prostrate bodies
> carpet His way.
>
> (*Orders have gone out to throttle
> Cassandra in her cell this night.*)

73

These youths and maidens are another turn on the inno-
cents sacrificed in war, and this colossus is war wrought to
its uttermost:

COLOSSUS STRIDES. HIS INCANDESCENT SHADOW
TURNS CITIES INTO SMOKING RUBBLE.
FORESTS ARE ASHES. ONLY BONES
MARK THE COURSES OF DRIED RIVER BEDS.
THIS STATION IS SIGNING OFF FOR LACK OF ANY SURVIVORS.

From deep in the ruins of the city
a jukebox is playing:
". . . Praise Him all creatures here below.
Praise him above, ye heavenly host . . . "
The needle is apparently stuck in the groove.
"Praise Him above . . . above . . . above . . . "

A seething wind leaves lava bubbles in its wake.

Two poems back, Arnaut questioned whether the great
abbeys and churches would still be standing in our time;
the answer given by this poem is no—unless, perhaps,
prophets of nuclear destruction are treated as the sane
members of the human race. Unlike the end of the world
in Revelations, this apocalypse is brought about purely by
mankind and his technologically enhanced powers of de-
struction. This state of affairs is symbolized visually in "The
Brocken," in the shadow cast by the last survivor, an army
chaplain, Captain Mephistopheles:

He totters, sways, spreads wide his arms
to try to keep his balance.

A gigantic shadow, luminous and accompanied by
a rainbow nimbus,
cast on the cloud bank by the setting sun,
reflects his movements.
Even after he drops dead,
the glow seems to linger on a moment
before slowly fading out.

The sequence has alluded to *Faust* before (in "Scene: A
Bedside in the Witches' Kitchen," "The Prayers," etc.); here
the drunk chaplain is obviously a modern counterpart of

Goethe's Mephistopheles, who proclaims during Walpurgis Night[1] on the Brocken:

> I feel that men are ripe for Judgment-Day,
> Now for the last time I've the witches'-hill ascended:
> Since to the lees *my* cask is drained away,
> The world's, as well, must soon be ended.

In the late 1930s, before Hiroshima and Nagasaki but after the destruction of Guernica, Guthrie wrote a visionary section for "Instead of Abel" in which the imagery is very similar to that of "Apocalypse." The poem, "Postlude: For Goya," was one of the few collected in his late books and is the only poem to appear in both *Graffiti* and *Asbestos Phoenix*. (It closes the 1968 volume, at the end of a section devoted primarily to the Vietnam War.) In the earlier poem, however, there are some survivors who, despite all the destruction, might be able to hope that "because we fought, others will fight" and that "earth still holds / some traces of a destiny":

> This is not an end,
> only an interlude: after a while
> we will creep forth and search among the crevices
> for seeds and cover them with dust
> and try for tears to quicken them.
> Remember only this is not an end.
> We cannot win—though we perhaps have won
> if we can only believe
> that this is not the end.

"We cannot win" was added to the poem for *Asbestos Phoenix*; the version in *Graffiti* is closer to the spirit of *Maximum Security Ward*:

> Remember only this is not an end.
> We have won if we can believe
> that this is not an end.

Belief in a more humane order of things remains a distinct possibility, as long as people are willing to speak out

---

1. Scene 21, Bayard Taylor's translation.

and act to the best of their ability in the cause of liberty for all. The French anarchist Louise Michel, one of the leading spirits of the 1871 Commune of Paris, is presented in "The Red Virgin" as battling all her life "for a world with neither slaves nor masters." Guthrie links her to "our own Abe Lincoln" and to "our John Brown" in a rare moment of tolerance for the course of American history. She was a fighter, an orator, and an artist—a prolific writer in many genres—with an admirable openness to the beauties of the world:

> Deported to New Caledonia, half a world away,
> four months on shipboard in a cage, she writes
> not of the hardships but, like a child
> on a first journey, of all the wonders:
> the sea itself, fresh winds, the mighty storms—
> later of the birds and animals, insects,
> huge handsome spiders and curious plants.

As a living counterpart of the "Black" Virgin of Le Puy, this "red" virgin is appropriate for Guthrie's gamut of goddesses. (She has somewhat the same exalted status in this sequence that Mme Curie has in *Paterson*.) The extent to which she was admired can be gauged by the length of her funeral procession, evidently made up of such common people as the "workers in Poitou" who carried her at the age of seventy-five on their shoulders. In *Maximum Security Ward*, the participants in this procession all but speak across the years to those in the protest walk of the next poem, "People Walking."

Dedicated to M. L. Rosenthal, the poem is to some extent a response to his "army of the dull and lonely" in "To the Shades of Old-Time Révolutionnaires" (in *Blue Boy on Skates*) and to the title sequence of *Beyond Power*. This little sequence, like Guthrie's poem "Boul' Miche," sprang from the 1968 Paris riots, and Guthrie was replying in particular to the opening passage of the third poem:

> To take the world in hand,
> a hero's resolution:

76

<blockquote>
Forgive us,
we are not ready.
Out of modesty, out of history, out of fear,
we are not ready.
</blockquote>

Guthrie's people walking ("not marching") through the streets of Paris, on the other hand, are neither dull nor lonely—or if they are, it doesn't matter. And they may indeed not be able to take the world in hand, yet in their own way they are heroic. Living has not been wasted on them:

<blockquote>
These are good people.
They want Vietnam to be free
and Algeria and Greece to be free
And France and America and every other country in the
    world
to be free. It is as simple as that.
They don't believe that walking in the rain
will *make* them free. But what else can they do?
This will say they *want* them to be free.
</blockquote>

<blockquote>
These are good people. They do not believe
what they are told to believe. They remember for
    themselves
what they have learned and known.
Living is not wasted on them.
They are good and brave people.
They have faith without hope
or hope without faith, or both without either.
They see no virtue in being gullible.
</blockquote>

They "remember" Auschwitz, Belsen, Neuengamme, Madrid, Teruel, Guadalajara, "the retreat / across the Pyrenees, where they learned / all causes are lost causes." (See "Some of Us Must Remember" in *Asbestos Phoenix*.) They are a cross-section of professions, classes, nationalities, and creeds; they do not belong to the race of "sheep herded by glib lies that greed concocts" ("'Loin de Moi'"); nor are they Titans. In the words of "The Christoi," they are simply

<blockquote>
ordinary men differing from their neighbors
only by speaking out when others are keeping silent,
</blockquote>

by saying "No" when others are giving dull assent,
by looking at situations clearly
and acting, within their means, accordingly,
by branding lies as lies.

They convey their own brand of grace on Guthrie; as long as he walks with them—sees the world through their eyes— he too is brave and good; he too is innocent.

VI. "Dawn beyond all limit of horizon"

"'Visse, Scrisse, Amò'" offers the final proof that living has not been wasted on Guthrie. It counters his distress in "Inventory" at living a stranger's life and his bitter recognition in "'Loin de Moi'": "I cannot think / of anyone less me than I am." In their several ways this forty-fifth poem and the four following it propose immersion in art as the key to the success or failure of one's life and as an antidote to loneliness as powerful as the communal emotion pervading the preceding poem. We see this aesthetically exalted perspective at work in the opening lines of "'Visse, Scrisse, Amò,'" which offer a personal response to Stendhal's epitaph ("He lived, wrote, loved"):

> Me too. At random for the lives I lived.
> Whose? Mostly good ones in any case.
> At moments I have heard the opaque silence
> that Giotto knew, the rock's reply to rock,
> confirmed, made holy, by the sky. I have guessed
> how wood and copper, china, felt to Chardin's touch,
> have walked in quiet ranks with men and women
> willing to die for what they knew
> their dying could not save.

Such extraordinary moments of empathy with other sensibilities are as real as any other events in one's life. They extend the boundaries of the individual, isolated consciousness enormously; in the case of great works of art, they represent the only true communion with the dead. Hence the language of the poem borders on the mystical in passages reciprocal with, but so different in feeling from, "The Surf":

> Gamut of goddesses, tear-channeled cheeks
> and rough-hewn, yearning vulva of Rosmertha,
> mother, sister, mistress of the dead.
> Ishtar, Epona, I have drunk your milk and tears.

. . . cone of light in my eyes . . .
All this is happening.
Lazarus, remember? I asked you for my name . . .
Thanks for refusing me an answer.

Finis terrae . . .
Pen-Marc'h, horse's head.

. . . wandering among the stands of menhirs.
Some of them have eyes and concave cones
to mark the breasts
cups and crosses
The drizzle has set in again   The dead move freely here.
I might speak to them   Gulls
and cormorants already answer.

We have lived strangers' lives
in depths and breadths of worlds they lived
and died to make.

Rarely has the experience of mystery been so simply and effectively conveyed as in these lines, fusing so many different manifestations of the religious spirit with the hellish aspects of the ward, Guthrie's beloved Breton peninsula, and the legacy of artists. Those "strangers," who are also christoi and immortal in their art, make possible our own form of resurrection: "We have lived strangers' lives / in depths and breadths of worlds they lived / and died to make." Guthrie's "litany of the christoi" ranges, in this poem, from "the man who set his feel of deer / swimming a freshet / on the walls of Lascaux" and the bison painter of Niaux to Louise Michel, Stendhal, Shakespeare, Proust, Balzac, Dickens. At the end of the poem, the problem of "The Surf" as to who one is is resolved: "Marsyas, do you remember me? Ishmael. / Strangers? Selves! Blood brothers."

This happy identification—happy in spite of the shared suffering, and perhaps in part because of it—is important to "'And the Evening and the Morning . . . '" also. The profound internal journey the poet has just accomplished is matched by a no less symbolic escape from that barred, prisonlike bed. The poem has elements of a surrealist drama, complete with mumbling "Voices," stage—on which Marsyas is standing in a hospital bathrobe (see "The Flute")—and "A SHATTERING WHITE SILENCE" that "BLINDS AND BLOCKS OUT EVERYTHING." This symbolic death leads to the re-creation implied by the title, and we find Marsyas "talking to the self that he has more or less found." This self is, of course, many selves (the "beaucoup d'autres" of "Caduceus"): Marsyas, Merlin, Ishmael, Icarus—all still flayed, imprisoned, outcast, and drowned—together with the humblest christos, Yorick.

The artist's imagination is capable of embracing "many different kinds of black birds," as "Caduceus" puts it, and now Guthrie draws attention to works of art that reveal "Blessèd incongruities, / blends of majesty and bawdry, tenderness and horror— / and innocence." Let us digress for a moment and remember that the surrealist filmmaker is praised in "Masque for Luis Buñuel" for precisely similar achievements, his "incongruous clarities" and "lewd homilies in flesh and bone." And, as we have seen, one of the defining characteristics of the genre to which *Maximum Security Ward* belongs is its ability to attain clarity through the fusion and balancing of the most disparate materials. (In line with this, the "Masque" is obviously a mini-sequence within the larger sequence, covering a wide range of poetic materials and providing clues to the approach one should take to somewhat less fragmented poems—"Arnaut Daniel," for example—and to the book as a whole.) Without the rendering of life in its totality, no true understanding of its nature or meaning is possible; paradoxically, one aspect of that understanding is our ability to admit that some things are essentially beyond the bounds of purely rational thought. To return to the poem and the prose passage it incorporates, even an Einstein is willing to make such an admission: "the mysterious . . . the fundamental emotion that stands at the cradle of true art and true science . . . The experience of mystery . . . this knowledge and this emotion that constitute true religiosity."

In the preceding poem, we were granted an intimate look at the "experience of mystery" in the communion with the dead. The next poem, "Judgment Day," is on a more

81

rational plane: on *that* side, "no one able to reach and touch another / except to carry pestilence and doom"; on *this* side, the "radiant innocence" of the christoi and of *our* God, who "holds forth such awards / as only the very innocent could ever prize." One passage in the poem—and one of the most moving in the sequence—is absolutely imbued with the sweetness of this new-found innocence:

> My name is Marsyas. I played a flute.
> Forget that silly challenge. I played it best alone,
> sitting on a rock or sprawled on banks of wolf's-foot,
> checkerberries.
> A chipmunk now and then would sit up and listen,
> a rabbit froze, ears flat along its back,
> after a while went on with nibbling.
> A bluejay cocked its head and gave a squawk.
> Once a box-turtle opened up and stretched
> its wattled neck in my direction.
> Nothing of an Orpheus about me. Not charmed,
> only at length reassured that this beast with
> its different kind of noise
> was as harmless as a nickering horse.

The response of the chorus of "Voices"—"Enough maundering"—is a built-in way of defusing accusations of sentimentality. But whereas the description of the killing of the snake in "By the Watch" or of the Walshes' view of heaven in "There Are Those" might be open to such a charge, this passage is beautifully pure. Its success, in fact, is probably responsible for Guthrie's reshuffling of his sequence so that "Judgment Day" could immediately precede "The Making of the Bear." (In the 1966–1967 draft the order of the closing poems, untitled in the cases of "The Flute" and "High Abyss" and in somewhat earlier versions, was "Judgment Day," "'And the Evening and the Morning,'" "The Flute," "The Red Virgin," "People Walking," two discarded poems ["Caliban Grown Old" and "Sealed Orders"], "'Visse, Scrisse, Amò,'" "The Making of the Bear," and "High Abyss.") In the final order, however, this thoroughly American scene of Marsyas among the checkerberries, having renounced his contest with Apollo and purged himself of humankind's more threatening attributes, prepares us for the extraordinary repossesion of a creative act performed some twenty millennia ago.

Through the simplicity of its language, "The Making of the Bear" suggests that it really does reflect the sensibility of the primitive artist intent on creating his masterpiece in the bowels of the earth. The poem, however, is a fable of the struggles and achievements of creative artists in any period, the creator of *Maximum Security Ward* not excepted. One of its most haunting images is the stone palimpsest that serves as this artist's easel:

> I edged my way along a slit so barred
> by stone icicles that I would have given up
> when, almost now in reach, I saw the wall
> that I have known since childhood
> yet never seen before. I saw it now
> even to the scratches other men,
> knowing the place for what it was, had made
> ages before me. Some of their animals were not
> like ours—one hairy beast with two horns on his snout
> was half glazed over by a layer of stone-ice.
> Many of them were drawn overlapping others—
> as mine would sprawl on theirs. None of them
> was anything the size that I intended.

In the case of this prehistoric christos, his innocent aspiration ("None of them / was anything the size that I intended") is completely justified, and the bear that he makes is not only true to life but so fully realized that it assumes the attributes of a totem animal ("When he began to breathe, / I stopped and snuffed the wick, safe in his / protection, slept"). Marsyas's edenic delight in the "banks of wolf's foot, checkerberries," and peaceful animals, Louise Michel's in the "huge handsome spiders and curious plants," Arnaut's in the budding willows and gentians, and the patient's in stubbled hillsides and brambled upland meadows are here embodied in the "living" bear the artist has created (the correlation with Burbank's horticultural creations is evident):

Heft, strength, the saddle and the soles,
the rambling appetite, fur, the rolling amble,
the curious, investigating "Whoof!"
the clatter of unretracting claws, the bear-play—
sliding on their rumps down clay banks into puddles,
standing erect and balancing vines across their noses—
patience to wait with poised paw
            on a rock among the rapids
to snatch the salmon as they leap,
the good
bear-smell of being bears
            are what I had tried to make the flint say
            on the cavern wall.

        Ferocity and gentleness . . .

The creation of the bear is an act of secret piety, and the pride is in the creation itself, not in the acclaim due such an artist: "No one will ever see him / but he still / is there." At the end of the book the competitive atmosphere, in which there is always a "winnuh and still champeen" who has overmatched one from the start, gives way to a more humble and ultimately grateful frame of mind. Thus Marsyas renounces the public challenge of Apollo, the maker of the bear works alone in the dark, and in the final poem, "High Abyss," a modern concertgoer admiringly uses Twain's distinction between the right word and the almost right one to distinguish between his vision and that of a titan:

I have come back having grasped perhaps as much
as a lightning bug, clinging through a storm
to a leaf's underside,
might understand by fellow-feeling
of the lightning stroke that in a single blast
has ripped the elm trunk all its length.

The work drawing the listener "into cyclone depths beyond me," effacing him "by vision more intense / than I could ever know," and lulling him "by a wild accord of warring energies" is Beethoven's String Quartet in C# Minor, op. 131. It is being re-created, however, not by titans of Beethoven's stature but by sweating men—one is lumpy and bald, with goldfish lips—and with quite ordinary materials:

> Four sweating men are drawing horsehair
> across squills of lamb gut and silver wire—
> and give the resin credit too; it makes the squawk.
>
> Delirious order
> of the march of suns and comets.

Inescapably the sublime has its source in the human, and the mystery of the creative power at work in the collaboration among dead composer, living musicians, and rapt listener is religious at its core. In the next-to-last stanza, the poet is able to reconcile the vision induced by art of the highest caliber with the Walshes' more orthodox perspective:

>   Beyond . . .
> "Beyond beauty," as Wagner said
> Beyond analogy   Coherence beyond coherence
> Locus beyond space-time continuum
>   (Paddy . . . Mim . . .)
> Dawn beyond all limit of horizon.
>
> Four men bow woodenly, file off the stage
> taking their instruments, leaving the scores
> on racks behind them.

Following the description of Beethoven's vision of a "Dawn beyond all limit of horizon," conveyed through the superlative musicianship of the players, are three remarkably touching lines. Hovering over them are any artist's hopes for his own work once he has stepped permanently offstage. Like many poets, the four performers are adept in their own realm and awkwardly human otherwise. The scores of op. 131 remaining on the suggestively empty stage are from one point of view merely pieces of paper with squiggles on them; yet, with proper human intervention, they transport us beyond all ordinary bounds. Perhaps *Maximum Security Ward*, in a sense the score of Guthrie's life, can have somewhat the same effect—even if he humbly sees its relationship to the work of a titan such as Beethoven as that of the lightning bug to the lightning. "High Abyss" pulses with such hopes at the same time that it moves calmly toward its assertion of human creativity as the transcendent force in and justification for human life.

Here *Maximum Security Ward* comes to rest, the powerful psychological and physical pressures that set it in motion not so much removed as held at bay by a more inclusive, ordering vision of mankind's possibilities. The sequence offers no happy ending in the ordinary sense. Wars go on and bigotry remains, Mélusine does not write, nor is Marsyas-Guthrie released from the hospital young and healed and whole. Any miracles take place within the imagination, but they are no less real for that. *Maximum Security Ward* testifies to the exuberant resilience of the human spirit under the most appalling physical and mental conditions. Whatever doubts Guthrie may have had about the ultimate worth of his book, like all our most valuable works of art it too makes a tentative yet satisfying order out of the chaotic welter of experience, plumbing the heights and depths of the human soul and thus revealing to us "secrets for changing life."

Appendix: Order of the Sequence

Part 1

Part 2

Selected Bibliography

By Guthrie

A. Poetry

Trobar Clus. Northampton, Mass.: S4N Society, 1923.
A World Too Old. New York: George H. Doran, 1927.
The Legend of Ermengarde, as Homer Rignaut. Paris: Black Manikin Press, 1929.
Scherzo from a Poem To Be Entitled THE PROUD CITY. Hanover, N.H.: The Arts Press, 1933.
Graffiti. New York: Macmillan, 1959.
Asbestos Phoenix. New York: Funk and Wagnalls, 1968.
Maximum Security Ward: 1964–1970. New York: Farrar, Straus and Giroux, 1970; London: Sidgwick and Jackson, 1971.
Maximum Security Ward and Other Poems. Edited with an Introduction by Sally M. Gall. New York: Persea Books, 1984.

B. Novels

Marcabrun. New York: George H. Doran, 1926.
Parachute. New York: Harcourt, Brace and Company, 1928.

C. Other Books

Le rôle du corps électoral dans le gouvernement fédéral des Etats-Unis. Toulouse: Impr. du Sud-Ouest, 1922 (thesis for *doctorat en droit*).
Translator. *The Revolutionary Spirit in France and America*, by Bernard Faÿ. New York: Harcourt, Brace and Company, 1927.
Editor, with George E. Diller. *French Literature and Thought Since the Revolution.* New York: Harcourt, Brace and Company, 1942.
Translator. *The Other Kingdom*, by David Rousset. New York: Reynal and Hitchcock, 1947.
Translator. *The Republic of Silence*, compiled and edited by A. J. Liebling. New York: Harcourt, Brace and Company, 1947.

89

Editor, with George E. Diller. *Prose and Poetry of Modern France.* New York: Charles Scribner's Sons, 1964.

D. Articles

"An Open Letter to Sidney Hook." *The Dartmouth Quarterly* 2 (Spring 1948): 3–6.

"Sinclair Lewis and the 'Labor Novel.'" In *Proceedings* of the American Academy of Arts and Letters, National Institute of Arts and Letters, 2d. ser., no. 2, 68–82. New York, 1952.

"The Birth of a Myth, or How We Wrote 'Dodsworth.'" *Dartmouth College Library Bulletin*, n.s. 3 (April–October 1960): 50–54.

"Dilys Laing (1906–60)." *The Carleton Miscellany* 4 (Winter 1963): 9–13.

"French Language and Literature." In *The American People's Encyclopedia*, 269–75. New York: Grolier, 1970.

"Remembrance of Things Past (1913–1927)." In *The Lessons of the Masters: An Anthology of the Novel from Cervantes to Hemingway*, edited by Malcolm Cowley and Howard E. Hugo, 399–402. New York: Scribner's, 1971.

"Dream and Poem, 1968." *The Carleton Miscellany* 12 (Fall–Winter 1971–72): 2–8.

About Guthrie

A. Books

Diller, George E., ed. *Ramon Guthrie Kaleidoscope.* Lunenburg, Vt.: The Stinehour Press, 1963. (See below for particularly relevant contributions to this *Festschrift* on the occasion of Guthrie's retirement from the Dartmouth faculty. Guthrie disagreed with the accuracy of some of the reminiscences; his corrections are on file in the Dartmouth Archives.)

Gall, Sally M. "The Poetry of Ramon Guthrie." Ph.D. diss., New York University, 1976.

B. Articles

Cooke, Alan. "An Attempt on Ramon Guthrie's Bibliography." In *Kaleidoscope*, 143–49.

Cowley, Malcolm. "The Summer of 1923." In *Kaleidoscope*, 76–80.

———. *The View from 80*. New York: Viking, 1980.

Diller, George E. Foreword to *Kaleidoscope*, ix–xi.

Fitts, Norman. "Right After the War." In *Kaleidoscope*, 55–68.

Gall, Sally M. "Ramon Guthrie's Forgotten Book." *Modern Poetry Studies* 9 (Spring 1978): 55–78.

———. "Ramon Guthrie." In *Great Writers of the English Language*. Vol. 1, *Poets*, edited by James Vinson, 449–50. New York: St. Martin's, 1979.

———. "Ramon Guthrie." In *Dictionary of Literary Biography*. Vol. 4, *American Writers in Paris, 1920–1939*, edited by Karen L. Rood, 184–85. Detroit: Bruccoli Clark, 1980.

———. Introduction to *Maximum Security Ward and Other Poems*. Edited by Sally M. Gall (with a foreword by M. L. Rosenthal), xiii–xxi. New York: Persea Books, 1984.

Gamsaragan, Daria. "Ramon en haut-relief." In *Kaleidoscope*, 113–16.

Griswold, Roger. "Algiers 1944." In *Kaleidoscope*, 105–9.

Laing, Alexander. "Pain, Memory and Glory: The Poetry of Ramon Guthrie." *The Carleton Miscellany* 11 (Summer 1970): 2–11.

Marks, Matthew. "Reminiscences of Ramon Guthrie." In *Kaleidoscope*, 97–101.

Méras, Edmond. "Ramon Guthrie 1920–1922." In *Kaleidoscope*, 69–75.

Nichols, Stephen G., Jr. "Ramon Guthrie '71h." *Dartmouth Alumni Magazine*, January 1974, 47.

Pioro, Gabriel. "Ramon, mon ami." In *Kaleidoscope*, 110–12.

Rapf, Maurice. "The Part Which is Guthrie." In *Kaleidoscope*, 117–24.

Rosenthal, M. L. "Ramon Guthrie's Poetry." In *Kaleidoscope*, 30–36.

Rosenthal, M. L., and Sally M. Gall. "Continuities, Post-Confessional and Eclectic." Chapter 15 of *The Modern Poetic Sequence: The Genius of Modern Poetry*, 444–94. New York: Oxford University Press, 1983. (Pages 444–60 treat *Maximum Security Ward*.)

Seldes, George. "De Havilland Fours and Sinclair Lewis." In *Kaleidoscope*, 81–91.

Véza, Laurette. "Ramon Guthrie." *Etudes Anglaises* 20 (1967): 47–54.